LOVE & DEATH

LOVE IS STRONG AS DEATH.
— Song of Songs

G. LEGMAN

LOVE & DEATH
A STUDY IN CENSORSHIP

HACKER ART BOOKS
NEW YORK
1963

COPYRIGHT 1949 BY G. LEGMAN

Second Printing, 1963

PRINTED IN U.S.A. BY
QUICK LITHOGRAPHERS, INC., NEW YORK 12, N. Y.

INSTITUTIONALIZED LYNCH · 7

NOT FOR CHILDREN · 27

AVATARS OF THE BITCH · 57

OPEN SEASON ON WOMEN · 83

INSTITUTIONALIZED LYNCH

> Art fell on its knees. Pressure was put on the publishers ... English fiction became pure ... But at this point human nature intervened; poor human nature! when you pinch it in one place it bulges out in another, after the fashion of a lady's figure.
> — George MOORE
> *Confessions of a Young Man* (1886)

THE CENSOR'S unequivocal 'You must not!' is seldom answered with an equally uncompromising 'I will!' Ashamed to oppose the censor's morality, and afraid to contravene his authority, the writer's first reaction is to evade the censorship, to see what can be sneaked through, what can be gotten away with, what can be disguised just enough to pass the censor but not so much as to escape the audience.

Hypocrisy, equivoque, misdirection: these are the subterfuges to which censors are blind, upon which audiences smile. The bawdy word, the rebel thought, the concept still taboo: these the author backs in upon the stage, masked and muffled, with arrows tangled in their hair pointing all in fraudulent directions. Words, thoughts, ideas – all are punned upon, hinted at, symbolized, turned upside-down and acrosticked, acted out in idiotic mummery, and finally, for the benefit of the dullest, are lettered out in kindergarten style. Thus Shakespeare's 'Her very C's, her U's, 'n' her T's' (*Twelfth Night*, II.v.88), the meaning of which puzzles professors so much, audiences so little. When genius must stoop to the nursery subterfuge of spelling its tabooed word out, nothing is to be expected of lesser craftsmen in resisting the censorship of sex.

The author pauses before truth, one eye furtively upon the censor, the other leering at his audience. He gibbers, he capers, he thumbs his nose and fires off popguns, but the truth is not in him. Now, as in Isaiah's time, truth is fallen in the street, dragged back & forth in mud lest the censor see it. His integrity forfeit – pawned, gone & forgotten

LOVE & DEATH

— the author juggles nonsense before the censor's face, the sense of nonsense behind his back. He tips his audience the broad wink of the elliptical dash —— batters them clownishly on the head with a bladderful of asterisks, pokes them in the ribs with a knowing blank to represent *coitus inconsummatus;* takes up his castrated tale again with 'Later.....'

He is a writer. He is Prometheus. His is the guardianship of light. But fear infects him. And from leader — light bearer — he has fallen away to jester and dishonorable jape. Truth is falsified, falseness made more false, darkness dissipated not at all by his flameless fire.

What can be said for men of letters whose vindication of the basic human right to freedom of speech can rise no higher than piddling and surreptitious naughtiness, cocked snooks when the censor's back is turned? Only that this sort of humor is not undertaken by grown men strictly as humor, but rather as their resistance to an oppressive censorship, for the sheer éclat of twitting and out-witting it. That, as resistance, it is ineffective, is due primarily to its being scaled so very small. For pranks and paraphrase and token resistance have their limits, and these are quickly reached. Having buffooned it to the end of the censorship tether—and it is short—the only recourse for both artist and audience is transvaluation, displacement, the siphoning off of the suppressible urge for expression elsewhere.

What is the 'elsewhere' of sex? Religion suggests prayer. Psychiatry proposes sublimation. The man & woman in the street are interested in neither. Transvaluation requires a fully equivalent satisfaction substituted for that suppressed. A sanctity that would equivalue a lifetime of sex, in depth and intensity, is beyond reach of all but saints. Sublimation to this same degree is impossible in our culture to all save an enfranchised élite: the bridge-builders, war-makers, movie-actresses. A thousand men must die to write one general's name in history, ten thousand women be damned to neurosis to pay one actress' wage; a million lives sink in the mud of the Nile to build one pyramid, found one concert series, immortalize one ironmonger's name in philanthropy. Sublimation is not for the million — unless through self-sacrifice — seldom for the few.

Professional moral elements, busying themselves with censorship, prefer to believe that sex can be replaced by physical and emotional exertions measurably less violent than itself, such as calisthenics, cold baths, and bingo. The sinister absurdity of this pious hope is everywhere obvious. The one thing, and the only thing short of total **sub-**

MURDER

limation, that can replace sex has become increasingly familiar decade by decade since the general introduction of Puritan censorship about 1740, and has reached so gargantuan a stage of formal development all around us that reflection upon the possible next step is plainly terrifying.

There is *no* mundane substitute for sex except sadism. You may search the indexes to Krafft-Ebing, Ellis, Hirschfeld, Guyon, or any dozen sex scientists, but you will find no other human activity that can replace sex completely – *spurlos versenkt*. Narcissism, homosexuality, zoöphily: these are clearly misdirections of ordinary sexual acts toward biologically unsuitable recipients. Fetichisms in all their number seldom supersede sexuality, generally do no more than to excite to it by a deviant concentration upon one attractive feature – breast, hair, foot, buttock, or whatever – an interest usually spread over all. But sadism does substitute. It is complete in itself. It can dispense with all earthly relation to sex – can dispense even with orgasm – thus allowing its adherents publicly to preen themselves on the 'purity' of their ruthless delights.

Geoffrey Gorer, the foremost student of the Marquis de Sade, makes the literary connection very plain in his *Bali & Angkor*, 1936:

> In English literature we can trace a series of secular mythologies, or accepted beliefs . . . to-day in the ecstasies of sexual love and violence, or (to use a single word for both manifestations) in *thrills*. The various uses of this word in current speech are sufficiently indicative. People talk of the thrill of love, the aesthetic thrill, the religious thrill, the thrill of danger, the thrill of murder, of robbery, and sudden death. Unfortunately we believe in our mythologies instead of using them, a disastrous and most dangerous situation . . . especially as the law does everything possible to prevent people enjoying the heaven which is in their art so endlessly preached at them, so that most people are in a chronic state of unsatisfied sexual desire . . . What is particularly dangerous is that despite all the prohibitions of convention and law people do acquire sexual experience, and for the greater part, find out that they have been stuffed with lies, that though pleasant, it is no such lasting ecstasy and final solution as art would leave us to suppose; and then they are ready for the other half of our myth, **violence**.

LOVE & DEATH

It is no accident that the end of Restoration bawdry coincided precisely with the fullest flowering of literary sadism in England. The Elizabethans had wrung blood in plenty out of sex – in *Romeo & Juliet*, a 'love'-play, seven of the characters are carted off dead – but there was no dearth of lust. Times change. The elegant eighteenth-century littérateurs, Johnson and Pope, are famous equally for the sexual purity of their writing, the sadistic cruelty of their speech. Sex being forbidden, violence took its place.

First had come the martyrologies and revenger-dramas, more than a century before, then the pirate almanacs and highwaymen lives; but these gave way quickly to the more refined brutality of Richardson's *Pamela* and Walpole's 'Gothic' novel. The whipped, stripped, and humiliated heroine-victim died a thousand deaths before the public grew bored with her writhings, applauded her lampooning in *Northanger Abbey* and the *Ingoldsby Legends*. While in France the Marquis de Sade added sex to the Gothic pattern – and gained thereby a century of mixed obloquy and praise for the British 'sadism' he had merely borrowed – the Anglo-American public, still eschewing sex, turned to fiercer pleasures in the murder-mystery, adapted by Edgar Allan Poe from the pirate & highwaymen memoirs.

Examine the journalistic detail of the first murder-mystery, published in Philadelphia, 1841, in *Graham's Lady's & Gentleman's Magazine*:

> On a chair lay a razor, besmeared with blood. On the hearth were two or three long and thick tresses of grey human hair, also dabbled in blood, and seeming to have been pulled out by the roots . . .
>
> Of Madame L'Espanaye no traces were here seen; but, an unusual quantity of soot being observed in the fire-place, a search was made in the chimney, and (horrible to relate!) the corpse of the daughter, head downward, was dragged therefrom; it having been thus forced up the narrow aperture for a considerable distance [. . . Dr. Freud, please note]. The body was quite warm. Upon examining it, many excoriations were perceived, no doubt occasioned by the violence with which it had been thrust up and disengaged. Upon the face were many severe scratches, and upon the throat dark bruises, and deep indentations of finger nails, as if the deceased had been throttled to death.

MURDER

After a thorough investigation of every portion of the house, without farther discovery, the party made its way into a small paved yard in the rear of the building, where lay the corpse of the old lady, with her throat so entirely cut that, upon an attempt to raise her, the head fell off, and rolled to some distance. The body, as well as the head, was fearfully mutilated – the former so much so as scarcely to retain any semblance of humanity.

To this horrible mystery there is not as yet, we believe, the slightest clew.

This is legal. This is printable. This is classic. But would it be legal, would it be printable, would it be classic if, instead of the details of murder and death, Poe had substituted with equal artistic precision the details of that act out of which life emerges? Apparently not. His second murder-mystery involved a girl (pardon the expression) no better than she should be; but Gaboriau, Wilkie Collins, Dickens, and Doyle cleaned all that out. By the time the murder-mystery was reimported to America, about thirty years ago, it was entirely sexless. Only sadism and pleasure in death had stood the crossing.

Poe's great contribution had been the enheroing of the avenger instead of the criminal, and with this one significant sop to moral pose, literary murder became respectable. The reading public went on a century-long debauch of printed sadism to replace the sex notoriously absent in Victorian literature. (For weaker stomachs, with a religious turn, the ghost story simultaneously served up masochist terrors.)

This is not the place to study the nineteenth century's love of death: the delight in funereal pomp, the clerical and poetical gloatings over the death of little children – nothing to compare with our own daily newsphotos of dying babies and squashed dogs – the special Christmas numbers of household magazines, specially chock full of murder; the reprint after expurgated reprint (in eight volumes each) of Foxe's Book of Martyrs, the endless purified editions of the State Trials in twenty-guinea sets and penny chapbooks, with now & again a poetic *procès-verbal,* as in the twelve-fold necrophily of Browning's laundered 'masterpiece,' *The Ring and the Book:* 'telling the story of a hideous murder twelve times over,' the *Encyclopaedia Britannica* marvels, '... insisting upon every detail with the minuteness of a law report.'

Nowhere, so much as in contemporary fiction, has this movement to substitute sadism for sex progressed so far and become so blatant. Yet so pervasive and so disguised is this perversion — in the exact sense of the word — that, when attacked at all, literature is attacked today not as sadism and sex-hatred but as overstressed normality: as 'obscenity.'

•

TWO MASKS serve to cover our transvaluation of censored sexuality into sadism and literary lynch — the murder-mystery and the 'spirited' heroine. (More violent than either, the comic-book is reserved as yet for children.) The murder-mystery is still the more popular, and for that reason perhaps the more dangerous, but the two are not different in any integral respect. The 'spirited' heroine merely enacts openly the sadistic pursuit and ultimate flagellation and destruction that the murder-mystery generally expresses only in symbols: in an appeal that passes through the censorship of the conscious mind disguised as justice, disguised as an exercise in mental agility, disguised as light, 'relaxing' entertainment.

For the real victim in the murder-mystery of our much consumption — as George Jean Nathan has pointed out — is not the murder*ee* but the murder*er*. The murdered individual is seldom pictured as an object of sympathy. More likely he (or she) is described as a 'swine' who should have been killed off years before, and whose murderer should really be given the Nobel prize. This is done partly to pose a large number of enemies — in the jargon, 'suspects' — but to a greater degree in order not to excite any impulses of sympathy or tenderness in the reader, even for the victim; since the entire purpose of the murder book is to excite and satisfy quite different impulses.

By casting one living individual into the character of a murderer, he is thrown automatically outside the pale of humanity, and neither justice nor mercy need be shown him. He can be tracked down callously and with superhuman intelligence by the much-mannered detective with whom the reader is clearly expected to identify himself — except, perhaps, in the first few chapters, where he savors the details of the kill in the character of the killer. The inane mannerisms and exotic eruditions — more recently the mock-virile 'toughness' — of the detective-superman are solely intended (if their easing the writer's task be omitted from the consideration) to pose a high degree of superior individuality for him, and thus to increase the gratification and cer-

MURDER

tainty with which the reader will project himself into the detective personality. Naturally, this projectibility-coefficient is the measure of the length and financial success of the series in which the particular detective appears.

The reader *is*, then, the detective – the supra-legal avenger. The police, who might snatch his prey from his private vengeance to public justice, are endlessly depicted as flat-footed bunglers, utterly incapable of bringing a routine murder to solution. And merely through committing this single murder – seldom more, unless forced into them to cover his tracks – the detective's prey (that is to say, the reader's prey) is degraded from the right to mercy, and is hounded without a qualm to his public humiliation before the assembled characters in the last chapter and to his eventual and inevitable suicide on the last page. This final humiliation and/or life-for-a-life suicide has, of course, become standard in murder-mysteries as being easier to write, less anti-climactic, and more titillatingly violent than courtroom justice – such as it might be – might be.

This pattern degradation of the murderer-victim from the right to mercy, to justice, due process of law, or even a lousy cot in the county jail is the hallmark and, in fact, the definition of lynching – whether armchair or hilltop. It works on the important but seldom stated principle by which, for instance, we arrange to have lambs slaughtered for food: They are very pretty little animals, and their bleating is quite piteous, but they simply are not human and they simply do not count.

In the same way Germans were given to understand that Jews are not human and, as such, can properly be gassed, electrocuted, and incinerated wholesale. In precisely the same way we are thrilled by a newsreel of the burning to death of a Japanese before our eyes. It is merely necessary to propagandize us first into an acceptance of the non-human status of the Japanese. This done, our previously conditioned sympathy with the underdog or with the inhumanly treated human can be shoved beneath the surface, and we are then properly able to enjoy photographs of a Japanese lynched with a flammenwerfer or his skull denuded of flesh, fitted with a brass top, and used as a tobacco humidor. Naturally, similar photographs of the body of an American burned to death or so desecrated by a Japanese would still strike us as bestial and inhuman.

Through ignorance of the principle here involved, Northerners tend to assume a very superior attitude of deploring when confronted with the fact of the lynching of Negroes in the South. They tend to think of Southerners as a gang of barbarians and murderers, of their well-publicized gallantry as a mere archaic pose. Yet there are thousands – perhaps millions – of Southerners who, for the plain protection of their economic interest, prefer to think of the Negro as non-human, and of his lynching as no more culpable, really, than the squashing of a cockroach in a sink; and who would feel no more outrage to their gallant impulses in castrating, branding, or killing a Negro than a friendly Westerner feels in castrating, branding, or killing a bull.

We Northerners, in precisely the same way, can accept with vapid equanimity the instantaneous obliteration of a hundred thousand Japanese, Germans, Russians, Martians, or any other group designated as enemy non-humans (reserving, of course, the right to execute enemy generals for slapping or underfeeding our prisoners of war), Englishmen deal in precisely the same way with Hindus and Jews, and – to revert – the reading public deals in precisely the same fashion with the synthetic murderer in its murder-fantasies. There is no difference, unless it be that all but the murder-mystery reader have some excuse. He alone lynches in cold blood.

Observe his specific requirements, his calmness, tabulated by Mr. Stephen Leacock in the *Saturday Review of Literature* for July 8th, 1939. The world only a matter of months from the total conflagration of war, the Canadian humorist placidly congratulates himself thus:

> I am one of those who like each night, after the fret and worry of the day, to enjoy about twenty cents' worth of murder before turning off the light and going to sleep. Twenty cents a night is about the cost of this, for first class murder by our best writers. Ten-cent murder is apt to be either stale or too suggestive of crime.

Did you say 'relaxing'? Soporific! Murder-lullabies for grown-ups, like the Gebrüder Grimm's blood-thirsty folk-tales, their sex watered down and their blood-thirstiness jazzed up from Giambattista Basile's originals. Mr. Leacock's concluding bit of advice is also worthy of any compleat lyncher's consideration:

> Don't be afraid to hang the criminal at the end; better lay the story, if you can, in a jurisdiction where they hang them, because to us, the readers, the electric chair sounds too uncomfortable. But hanging is old and respectable . . . I mean

MURDER

we want him *hanged* [Mr. Leacock's italics]; don't let him fall into the sea out of his aeroplane. It's not good enough. Hold him tight by the pants till you get him to the gallows.

Mr. Leacock is presumably kidding, but his bare-naked, unexpurgated accents of bloodlust would be printable even if – as one may suspect – he was entirely serious. The murder-mystery reader feels no shame, cannot see himself for the super-murderer that he patently is. His murderer-victim kills just once. He, the reader, kills three hundred times a year – daily except Sunday – generally just before going to sleep. 'First class murder by our best writers.'

•

ONE UNDERSTANDS that the murder-mystery is a sort of intellectual puzzle, 'mental exercise' for mentalities too dim or too jaded for the symbolic combats of cross-word puzzles and chess. But why, then, this persistent, pathological paddling in guts & blood? Why this intense, invariable, I-am-the-man insistence upon personal vengeance in a culture where revenge is disgraceful, the taking of the law into one's own hands a crime? Why must it be murder, murder, murder, murder?

Are there no other mental exercises than the contemplation of death? Not for the mystery-reader. In 1926, the year that the 'detective' mystery mushroomed into prominence in America, E. M. Wrong, its first serious apologist, found it necessary to record that:

> Time has ... exalted murder, which used to be only one of several offences, to a position of natural supremacy.
>
> There are good reasons for this. What we want in our detective fiction is not a semblance of real life, where murder is infrequent and petty larceny common... Hatred that is strong enough to bring murder is familiar enough to be intelligible to nearly every one, yet far enough from our normal experience to let us watch as detached observers [!] for we do not feel that it is our own crimes that are unmasked. So for many reasons murder is advisable, though not necessary. The author, if he withholds its appeal, must give us compensation in some other way.

(The Oxford University Press, that publishes Mr. Wrong's little anthology of murder – in its 'World's Classics' series – simultaneously offers for sale an expurgated Herrick and a bowdlerized Shakespeare. What is the 'compensation in some other way' that readers of Oxford's desexualized Herrick and Shakespeare are supposed to seek?)

Twenty years ago – despite Mr. Wrong's manifesto – the 'mental exercise' whitewash might still have held some drops of water. Today the Who-Stole-the-Necklace-or-The-Mystery-of-the-Butler's-Past sort of milk & mush is a drug on the market, and even the most apologetic of the British enthusiasts do not absorb it in any number. The international *Cumulative Book Index* tries to distinguish only between 'detective' murders and murders merely mysterious, attempting no category for mysteries based on crimes other than murder. For that matter, murder is generally less gruesome than the 'compensation in some other way' – impending death, plague, or unspecified doom threatening all of humanity or even London – that writers of the non-lethal mystery see fit to bring in. It is, in any case, a vanishing form, and any possible *bona fide* in the 'mental exercise' defense has vanished with it.

Even fifteen years ago, when Harry Stephen Keeler (and 'Ellery Queen') created murders with the solution sealed, announcing that all the clues had been given and that the reader should be able to logic out the murderer's identity, no one wanted to bother and this feature was quickly dropped. That readers commonly abort the whole 'mental exercise' angle, and sneak a glimpse at the solution beforehand, is so well known that writers are hard put to it to think up tricks to forfend them – like making the narrator the murderer, and having the denouncement narrated by someone else. The reader-pack yelps. "Who Cares Who Killed Roger Ackroyd?" They care. They want to know *who* they are hunting down. Though the murder-mystery is ostensibly a glorification of law & order ('Crime does not pay' and so forth) the reader wants to cheat while reading it. How now, mental exercise?

Make no mistake about it: the murder-mystery reader is a lyncher. A solid citizen by day, by night he rides hooded to watch human beings die. He may, certainly does, think of himself as a mere, harmless literary escapist. He may actually believe that his nightly passion to murder the murderer of his own creating adds up to nothing more than pleasant, law-abiding, purely meaningless recreation – light entertainment, and all that. He may imagine that the mental torture, the anxiety, the pounding heart and terror (*jargonicè*, 'suspense'), the desperate twistings & turnings, and the final, ingeniously contrived hu-

MURDER

miliation and death of the murderer — three hundred violent and excited pages of it — all these, he may imagine, are no part of his interest.

Yet remove from the murder-mystery this element of sadism — of manhunt and lynch — and what is left? A flabby mush of greed, mistaken identity, or vernacular chit-chat. Wholly without attraction for nine in every ten readers, the non-lethal mystery does not sell, is not read, and is now therefore seldom encountered. *The* 'mystery' is the murder-mystery. And the murder-mystery reader wants blood, death, and lynching. But not the blood of the 'victim,' whose unwept death — presumably the whole justification for the protracted lynch that follows — is lackadaisically presented on page one as a *fait accompli,* an utterly routine knock-down-&-drag-out bit of ritual. The murder-mystery reader wants the murderer's blood.

And again, where is the difference? The murderer may have killed from the noblest of motives. His 'victim' may have been a blackmailer, a drug-peddler (of anything but alcohol), a sadist (*sic*), a human ghoul. It may all even have been a mistake. But what are the reader's motives? He has none. He is quite calm. His interest in law & order is infinitesimal — so much so, that he enthroned the murder-book as our prime literary fare (one third of all fiction printed) in the midst of the illegal, nation-wide whiskey-jag of the 1920's. The murders that he avenges are written to order for him. Wholly synthetic, they would not exist at all but for his endless thirst for blood. He picks up his nightly 'mystery,' prepared to lynch down whatever miserable murderer his author chooses to present. He is unprejudiced. He has no personal grudge. He will kill *any*body. He kills for pleasure.

It may be pointed out that, in this, murder-mystery *aficionados* differ in no way from the readers of newspaper accounts — voyeurism at second hand — of courtroom trials and executions. This is certainly true. William Bolitho's definition of the murder trial (in *Murder for Profit,* 1926, page 3) might with equal propriety be applied to the murder-mystery, for both, equally, are

> the celebration of a human sacrifice by suffocation, to which modern men are excited in a crowd by the recital of some bloody deed whose details awaken hate and fear to which the coming execution is the fore-shadowed, fore-tasted complementary. Everything there . . . is devised to create that hoarse atmosphere in which alone modern men, in a state of peace, can work themselves up to a corporate killing.

It may even be pointed out that the human sacrifice of, and to, the murderer in books – three hundred of them a year, every year (not counting reprints) with an audience in millions – appeals to the same socially accepted bloodlust as that thought desirable at prize- & bull-fights. This, also, is true. It might be questioned, however, whether the lulling along of these death-pleasure emotionalisms through symbolic satisfaction in books and arenas does more than to keep them ever-fresh in the race, waiting only for the stress of economic struggle, religious factionalism, and war to free them from the limitations of symbolism and scapegoatry, and allow them brutal and delighted play.

●

THERE IS a sort of Gresham's Law by which bad art drives out good. Murder having replaced sex in the popular arts, the glorification of one requires the degradation of the other. Death calls down anathema on love. Pronouncing judgment on March 29th, 1948, in the Winters case, the Supreme Court of the United States of America all but declared, as its studied decision – re-argued three times in as many years – that so far as art and literature are concerned, sex is worse than murder.

This stupefying pronouncement is now the law of the land, and will remain so probably for decades. For all practical purposes it has always been the law. The New York Penal Law § 1141(2) – now struck down by the Supreme Court – which made literary 'bloodshed' at least as bad as sex, has been a dead letter for over half a century, nullified and ignored ever since it was passed in 1884 in New York and in twenty-three other states since.

Meanwhile, the anti-obscenity subsection (1) of the same law is still very much alive. Thousands of persons have been prosecuted, and most of them fined or imprisoned, under this subsection and the Postal Law similar – which triples the penalty for obscenity, but neglects to mention 'bloodshed' at all. But it would be difficult to find more than three solitary cases in these last sixty-five years – *Strohm,* 160 Illinois 582; *McKee,* 73 Connecticut 18; and now *Winters,* 294 N. Y. 545 – prosecuted anywhere in the country for the publication of 'pictures, or stories of deeds of bloodshed, lust or crime.' In the face of disinterest such as this, the Supreme Court's decision is merely the catching up of the law with the national temper.

MURDER

The error in the inferior court, that brought the Winters case to the Supreme Court in the first place, had been the gratuitous interpretation of the law as requiring the stories or pictures of bloodshed &c. to be 'so massed as to become vehicles for inciting' to crime — the purpose being to ban murder-magazines without banning books. Nevertheless, so great (according to the Supreme Court) are the legislative powers of the judiciary, that this mere statement by an inferior court 'puts these words in the statute as definitely as if it had been so amended by the legislature.' And, on the principal ground that the New York Penal Law § 1141(2) had been thus 'amended' into ambiguity, the original laws of twenty-three other states were declared unconstitutional. *Fiat justicia.*

This retroactive hanky-panky is not, however, half so significant as the fact that, and the illogic with which, simultaneously, the prohibition against obscenity was affirmed:

> The impossibility [says the Supreme Court] of defining the precise line between permissible uncertainty in statutes, caused by describing crimes by words well understood through long use in the criminal law — obscene, lewd, lascivious, filthy, indecent or disgusting — and the unconstitutional vagueness that leaves a person uncertain as to the kind of prohibited conduct — massing stories to incite crime — has resulted in three arguments of this case in this court. (333 U. S. 518.)

This is, of course, clear warning — twice repeated — that the Supreme Court majority fully intends to find the obscenity law (1) constitutional when it comes finally to be argued before it, though it has found the 'bloodshed' law (2) unconstitutional. It does not matter. The prejudice clearly apparent behind the foreground technicalities of the Winters decision is, after all, the national opinion as well: that sex in literature is worse than murder. In life, however, the situation is the reverse. So that we are faced in our culture by the insurmountable schizophrenic contradiction that sex, which is legal in fact, is a crime on paper, while murder — a crime in fact — is, on paper, the best seller of all time.

It therefore does not matter in the least what the Supreme Court decides concerning sex. It is not law that keeps the censorship going. The Comstocks, the Sumners, the virgin sex-experts of the Catholic Church (and the postal inspectors they control) — even the liberal lawyers who expurgate books beforehand for our pusillanimous publishers – these are not the censor. The American censorship of sex is internalized. The men & women in the street carry it around with them in their heads. *They* are the censor, and to the degree that the law mirrors their wonted censorship, the law can be enforced and will be obeyed. Where the law diverges from the *mores* of the times – in our time, the substitution of an allowable sadism for a censored sexuality – the law is worthless and unenforceable.

The proof of this will be in the sequel to the *Hecate County* fiasco, in which – the first obscenity case since Winters' to reach the Supreme Court (October 25th, 1948) – the law was silently upheld in a tie vote. No one imagines that if sex should be exonerated by the Supreme Court, in a moment of headlong consistency, obscenity would for a moment become legal. No one is so foolish as to think that if the obscenity laws of the states, Post Office, Federal Communications Commission, and Customs combined should be declared unconstitutional, pornography could be openly published in the United States, as bloodshed, bloodlust, and crime are published.

Hardly. New laws would be passed overnight, avoiding whatever technical errors might cause the present obscenity laws to fall. The legislative courage might even be found to abandon the multiple and 'permissible' uncertainty of meaningless adjectives like 'obscene, lewd, lascivious, filthy, indecent or disgusting' – saying nothing, in their overlapping terror, but that they are afraid – and to set up frank and objective criteria of guilt: that (with, of course, the usual exceptions for technical treatises, 'detective stories ... reports of battle carnage, &c.' – *verbum sat sapienti*) the description of sexual relations of any kind, or of the genital organs of either sex, in text or in pictures, is a crime; or–if safety is still to be sought in subjectivity–that any passage of text, or any picture, that gives seven of twelve good men & true an erection is, by that test, criminal.

On the other hand, let new laws against the exploitation of literary bloodshed now be passed – even under the subterfuge of protecting children, and in all the wordings and with all the preambles that Justice Felix Frankfurter's minority opinion carefully indicates such laws must have if they are not to fall before the Supreme Court as § 1141(2) has fallen – and what, precisely, will be achieved? A new dead letter, a new unenforced and unenforceable law, will have been written on the books of half, or perhaps this time all, the states. The Postal Law, which punishes obscenity as a crime where the states find

MURDER

it only a misdemeanor, might even see its way clear to banning literary bloodshed too – something it has never yet thought to do. Three cases might possibly be prosecuted in the next sixty-five years, during which prosecutions the professional liberals of the American Civil Liberties Union and the Authors' League can be expected to pop up, *amicus curiae*, to assail this unbearable restraint of free speech. Meanwhile, the staggering amount of sadism in all our pulp- & pocket-literature will rise from its present thousands of tons yearly to millions, from its present fifty percent or more to the intended saturation point of one hundred and one – Aldus' incunabular dream of popular classics come true as a nightmare.

●

WITH THE exception of C. Day-Lewis ('Nicholas Blake') and Donat O'Donnell, who know what a murder-mystery is – and why – Mr. Howard Haycraft and his assembled experts in *The Art of the Mystery Story* (1946) – likewise Miss Barbara Howes and hers, in *Chimera*, Summer 1947 – confess themselves frankly puzzled as to why, except for the money in it, they write about murder, and why anybody wants to read about it. Their provisional solution, and apology, seems to be that human beings naturally lust after blood, and that the murder-writer is a sort of literary pimp, who serves the socially useful purpose of giving vicarious satisfaction on paper to this natural urge, thus keeping it from finding expression in lethal fact.

That 'mystery' writers are murder-pimps would be hard to gainsay. But the presumption that we, all of us, have some 'natural' component of bloodlust is presumption indeed. We have nothing of the sort. No animal kills for pleasure alone. But – we do have our frustrations. We do have our fears. We all have our inadequacies: sexual, economic, and personal. And it is for these that the prize-fight, the fox hunt, the sports page, tabloid, comic-book, and murder-mystery supply a safe, cheap, socially water-tight solution: institutionalized amok.

Are you impotent, frigid? Does your wife insult you in bed, your husband dominate you? Why get a divorce? Divorce is expensive – for Catholics, impossible. A murder-book is only ten cents to borrow, twenty-five cents to own – free, gratis & for nothing to write. Strangle your spouse nightly on paper. (The murder-mystery is the foundation of the family: it prevents divorce.) Does your boss tyrannize and exploit you? Don't shoot him – you'll hang for it. Kill him nightly on paper – you the detective, he the hounded-down murderer. (The murder-mystery is the mainstay of usury: it prevents revolution.) Are you weak, stupid, namby-pamby, ineffective? Don't improve yourself. Don't turn against your constricting, recalcitrant environment. Dissipate the aggression you feel, siphon off your endocrine resources, be a killer, nightly – three hundred nights a year – for a dollar a week. Absurdly simple, cheaper than a hunting license, and you hunt human beings. (The murder-mystery is the backbone of civilization: it dispenses utterly with intelligence.)

Human blood in the gladiatorial arena kept Roman slave hordes satisfied with their dole of bread. *Panem et circenses*. Not by bread alone does man live. He needs blood spilled before his eyes, too, or he may want butter on that bread. Next after fire, the murder-mystery is society's most valuable servant. Without it, there might be some changes made.

Optimistically, perhaps, the Right Reverend Monsignor Ronald Knox finds the murder-mystery 'in danger of getting played out.' (*The Tablet*, London, Xmas 1946, vol. 188: page 355.) And modestly, as becomes the author of *The Viaduct Murder, The Body in the Silo*, &c. &c. – and, between murders, Bible translator and domestic prelate to His Holiness the Pope – Monsignor Knox adds:

> Nobody can have failed to notice that while the public demand remains unshaken ... the means of writing [a 'detective mystery'] with any symptom of originality about it, becomes rarer with each succeeding year. The game is getting played out ... the stories get cleverer and cleverer, but the readers are getting cleverer ... too.

Perhaps. But Monsignor Knox is misled. The literary quality of the murder-mystery has nothing to do with its sales. The murder-reading public is not hungry for style; it is thirsty for blood. The puzzle element, the cleverness of writers or audience, the word 'mystery' itself – all are simply frauds: pretty lamb-chop panties of paper with which genteelly to grab hold of the raw meat of sadism. The problem, however, is not one of wilful pathology. The literate population of Great Britain and America is not largely composed of fantasy-sadists out of malice prepense. They cannot help themselves.

MURDER

Nor are they comfortable in their uncontrollable letch for death. A gnawing guilt disturbs them. And they must dither and blather, refer nervously to 'the search for certainty in an uncertain world,' to 'puzzles,' to 'pattern,' and plain 'addiction.' They must write yearly defenses – with no attack ever yet published. They must point with anxious pride to kings and lesser fry (the frustrated do-gooders: Lincoln, Wilson, Roosevelt) sharing their lethal 'relaxation,' to an *arbiter homicidiarum* hustling a murder-library into the White House, to a Catholic priest with five murder-mysteries 'to his credit' and a Marxist critic ('Caudwell'-Sprigg) with six, to the titubating comedy of a titled English philosopher carving up a Christmas pudden of self-congratulation for himself and the other 'mystery'-fanciers of Great Britain with the nincumpoop suggestion that reading about murder will 'realise ... the unification of mankind' and 'abolish war.' (Lord Bertrand Russell, in *The Listener,* Xmas 1948, vol. 40: page 1010.)

Least innocent, because they are most aware, are the amateurs of murder – the writers especially – the feuilletonist clergymen, the pansy intellectuals, the homicidal housewives and pseudonymous college-professors, all swilling happily through paper straws at their hot cathartic toddy of blood. Least guilty, because stupidest, are the professionals – the word-mongers: publishers and their hacks – hip-deep in murder strictly for the dollar, the merest puppets of their *Zeitgeist.* And they will tell you that only the public is responsible, only the reader-mass is culpable. And yet, are even these to blame?

The frustrations implicit in twentieth-century life, that make necessary our diet of murder, have not been resolved and cannot be resolved within the framework of our profit-economy and anti-sexual morality. Love being unwholesome, and revolution unhealthy, only one petcock of release is left us: we may dream of violence, of death; watch it in arenas, quiver over it on paper, run amok in fantasy, identifying ourselves always with the killer, the killer of killers – the superman. Our need is acute. The demand is paramount. And blood and death and violence will therefore continue to be supplied.

•

LIKE THE Talmudic pig, holding up its cloven forefeet from the dung-wallow where it lies, grunting 'Clean! I'm clean!' murder-writers and readers are anxious to demonstrate that at least their feet are kosher: there is no sex anywhere to be seen. (The exceptions, and what they actually prove, will be considered later.) Absorbed in their obedience to the Sixth Commandment – the one against killing – reminding themselves nightly of its sinfulness, they would view with consternation the proposal that, simultaneously and by similar means (let us say three hundred juicily-titled pornographic novels yearly, all ending with horrible punishment in the venereal ward), society might show its reverence for the Seventh. No. This goose and this gander require different sauces. Literary murder is respectable, 'relaxing,' anything you please. Literary sex – it doesn't even have to be adultery – is 'obscene.'

Mr. Rex Stout, who opines (in Howard Haycraft's cynically-titled centenary, *Murder for Pleasure: The Life & Times of the Detective Story*, 1941, page vii) that 'people who don't like mystery stories are anarchists,' warily announces over the radio that if 'by romance... you mean love... I'm out of it. I'm a writer of murder-mysteries and I'm not supposed to know anything about it.' (The Author Meets the Critics, December 5th, 1946.) Naturally, Mr. Stout, naturally. When 'our best writers' are profitably peddling murder, and our best critic, Edmund Wilson, is barely escaping jail for 'obscenity,' who wants to bother with love?

In the midst of death, love is no part of our dream. Our imaginations stuffed with murder, we are too moral for sex. Drugged on blood and death, murder upon murder, two abreast, three hundred deep, year after bloody year; killing for the pure lust of killing – for the lack of courage to rebel; usurping, in the name of justice, the prerogatives of all justice, human & divine; our multi-millions of 'mystery' readers *prefer* their transvalued pattern – empty of sex, reeking with sadism – within the boundaries of which, as it would seem, no one dares to attack them.

NOT FOR CHILDREN

NOT FOR CHILDREN

THE AMERICAN generation born since 1930 cannot read. It has not learned, it will not learn, and it does not need to. Reading ability just sufficient to spell out the advertisements is all that is demanded in our culture. With only token recourse to the printed word, for more than a decade the radio, the talking movie, the picture-magazine and comic-book have served all the cultural and recreational needs of the generation of adults now upon us. For them, the printed word is on its way out.

Increasingly, in the last century, sadism has been supplied to the American public in massive doses in all its popular arts until, now, one out of every three trees cut down in Canada for paper-pulp has murder printed on it when the presses roll. The frustrations – sexual and economic – that this printed violence has been siphoning off, will obviously not disappear along with the ability to read. And so, new aural and visual media have been prepared, primed to replace the murder-mystery and 'action' pulp now turning dim before the eyes of a growing nation of illiterates. Whole industries have sprung up based ultimately on the exchanging of printed death for pictorial. The murder movie, the radio horror show, the bloody sports that have put television over, the disaster headlines of the daily tabloids and the photographic agonies of the weekly, *Life* [sic] and its various imitators, all are chomping at the bit – ready, willing, and anxious to purvey 'cathartic' violence to trapped millions. The kiddies' korner in this new national welter of blood is the comic-book. The hood, the disguise, the Ku Klux promise of immunity: 'entertainment.'

The aggressive content of comic-books is so conspicuous that most observers fail to notice that this aggression is rigidly channelized, that the willingness of any reader to accept a fantasy escape from his frustrations presupposes a willingness to achieve something less than total and actual escape. Like all other forms of dreaming, literature operates under a censorship. And this censorship – in both its legal and internalized expression – does not allow any direct, total attack on the frustration that elicits the dream. It offers a choice. Either the attack must restrict itself to something less than an attack, to partial and symbolic aggressions, or its object must appear in disguise.

In practice this adds up to a choice between fantasy attacks on real frustrations, and real attacks on fantasy frustrations. This is also the difference between comic-strips and comic-books: not to be confused. The strips published in newspapers are for adults, and concentrate on real enemies – husbands, wives, bosses, policemen, and civilized pressures in general. With equal realism, they restrict this attack to mere permissible comedy – to pranks, jeers, and naughtiness: token resistance.

The comic-*books* are for children, and their content is totally that of dreams. They concentrate on impossibly real aggressions – impossible under civilized restraints – with fists, guns, torture, whips, and blood. Meanwhile, the dream-censorship respectabilizes this attack by directing it against some scapegoat criminal or wild animal, or even against some natural law like gravity, rather than against the parents & teachers who are the real sources of the child's frustration and therefore the real objects of his aggression.

Children are not allowed to fantasy themselves as actually revolting against authority – as actually killing their fathers – nor a wife as actually killing her husband. A literature frankly offering images for such fantasies would be outlawed overnight. But, in the identifications available in comic-strips – in the character of the Katzenjammer Kids, in the kewpie-doll character of Blondie – both father and husband can be thoroughly beaten up, harassed, humiliated, and degraded daily. Lulled by these halfway aggressions – that is to say, halfway to murder – the censorship demands only that in the final sequence Hans & Fritz must submit to flagellation for their 'naughtiness,' Blondie to the inferior position of being, after all, merely a wife. In other words, the *status quo* must be restored in some perfunctory genuflection as the reader leaves. This is the contract under which direct-attack fantasy is allowed: the attack must be incomplete; even so, being against authority, it must be punished; and, in the last analysis, it must change nothing.

Obviously this is unsatisfactory. Adults, habituated to compromise, can make their peace with it, but for children it is apparently intolerable. Not only the degree of allowed violence is much too low, but the final punishment reinstates, as it is meant to reinstate, precisely the situation the child is trying to escape from. Children's literature, therefore – the really popular children's literature: Grimm's

NOT FOR CHILDREN

Fairy Tales, the expurgated *Arabian Nights,* Foxe's *Book of Martyrs,* and now the comic-book – traditionally takes the other alternative, disguising the hated parent and feared authority (necessarily sacrosanct) as a witch, an ogre, a pirate, Red Indian, clay duck, criminal, martyr, spy, saboteur, 'mad' scientist, or other human sacrifice condemned to death by definition; and in this way becomes free to enact upon him – or her – a really satisfactory degree of violence. At the same unconscious level that the reader identifies himself with the heroic avenger, he may also identify whoever has been frustrating him with the corpse.

Violence displaced in this way from its intended object invariably appears in larger and larger doses, more and more often repeated. Little trapped people, who have no other medicine but the wrong one, can be expected to take more and more of it, to still the growing realization that they will never be cured that way. At this point, what was intended as social antisepsis becomes pathology. Not knowing, or not being able to admit that they are fobbed off with scapegoats, children are nevertheless aware that their transvalued violence does not satisfy them. They keep asking for more. Increase the dose! Fifteen years ago, in 1933, there was not one comic-book openly published in the United States. Today, at a conservative estimate, there are five hundred million yearly: three hundred titles or more, each with an average monthly printing of two hundred thousand copies. From zero to half a billion yearly, in fifteen years – the greatest, fastest literary success the world has ever seen.

●

THE HISTORY of the comic-book has not yet been traced. Its descent can be roughly seen in the bison-drawings of the cave-dwellers, the hieroglyphic writing of Egypt (in which the *cartouche,* or conversation-balloon, first appears), the architectural friezes of Babylonia, Central America and Indonesia, the ceramic decorations of Greece, the silver-chasing of Roman arms and armor, the wall *graffiti* of Pompeii (and compare our own), the hunting tapestries of the Middle Ages, the playing-cards, fortune-telling Tarot and pious block-books of the Renaissance, the woodcut Dances of Death of 15th century France, the horizontal scrolls *(makimono)* and picture-books of Japan, the crowded canvases of the Flemish peasant painters **Breughel, Brouwer, and Bosch.**

LOVE & DEATH

The modern comic-book had been achieved in Hogarth's *Harlot's Progress* (1732), in Rodolphe Töpffer's *'Histoires'* – pirated in the 1840's as the first American comic-books *(American Notes & Queries,* 1946, vol. 5: page 149) – and, full color and all, in *The Fools Paradise* published by Hotten in London about 1873; but only the strips flourished until the 1930's. There, in the private lynchings of detective 'Dick Tracy' and 'Secret Agent X-9' (by way of Edgar Allan Poe), the interplanetary paranoia of 'Buck Rogers' and 'Flash Gordon' (H. G. Wells' *War of the Worlds,* 1898) and the loincloth cavortings of 'Jungle Jim' (Edgar Rice Burroughs' *Tarzan,* 1914), a formula was evolved that restored the comics to children at least on Sundays – the daily strips having been abandoned by them to adults a decade before, as too unbearably tame.

Im tiefsten Depressionszeit, with money-anxieties and the fear of war hanging over the American mind, it was not difficult to peddle a cult of death, with the reader finding identification naturally in the topmost killer. Murder-mysteries boomed. Cowboy pulps blossomed, in both their western and interplanetary avatars. And for children, the Mars and crime and jungle strips showed that it was possible to get beyond Mr. Hearst's Katzenjammer Kids and their pea-shooter (plagiarized to order from Wilhelm Busch's 'Max und Moritz,' half a century before), and really handle guns and blood.

By 1936, before anyone had even heard of the comic-books then preparing, a sociologist could find the Sunday strips 'catering to neurosis,' offering 'escape to a morbid imagery and brutal sadism' (Aaron Berkman, in *American Spectator,* 1936, vol. 4: page 53), while from the Catholic University in Washington came this resumé of the contents of, mind you, strips:

> Sadism, cannibalism, bestiality. Crude eroticism. Torturing, killing, kidnaping . . . Monsters, madmen, creatures half-brute, half-human. Raw melodrama; tales of crime and criminals . . . pirate stories . . . emphasis upon cruelty, human torture, horrible forms of death, human sacrifice . . repetition in word and picture of . . . bestial and degenerate scenes. . . . (John K. Ryan, in *Forum,* 1936, vol. 95: pages 301-304)

with a few bitter animadversions on the spectacle of the Supreme Court of the United States sitting gravely upon the 'momentous issue, who would purvey these scenes to the people of the District of Columbia,' in bland disregard of the principle that contestants must come into court with clean hands, that there can be no equity in a *prima facie* immoral act.

Then came the comic-books, the secret of their unprecedented success – if anything can be called a secret that appears in sixty million copies monthly – being, of course, their violence. All comic-books without exception are principally, if not wholly, devoted to violence. And just as the murder-stories for the use of frustrated adults are politely euphemised as 'mysteries,' just so the yearly half-billion violence-leaflets for children are camouflaged as 'funnies,' as 'comics,' as 'jokes,' though there is never anything comical in them.

Garishly presented in clashing colors, and cheaply printed in forty-eight pages of paper-bound pulp with even more garish covers, what recourse there is in comic-books to the printed word is, totally, language violence: full capitals throughout, bold-face accents liberally besprinkled, and exclamation points galore; with illiterate little cartouches, where no conversation is thought necessary, saying Pow, Zow, and Whammo! to indicate the administration of violence, while the victims respond with Awrrk, Aagh, Aieee, Ooof, and Uggh.

The price being only ten cents apiece, and the distribution national, every American child can and does read from ten to a dozen of these pamphlets monthly, an unknown number of times, and then trades them off for others. If there is only one violent picture per page – and there are usually more – this represents a minimum supply, to every child old enough to look at pictures, of three hundred scenes of beating, shooting, strangling, torture, and blood per month, or ten a day if he reads each comic-book only once. The fortification of this visual violence with precisely similar aural violence over the radio daily, and both together in the movies on Saturday, must also be counted in.

With rare exceptions, every child in America who was six years old in 1938 has by now absorbed an absolute minimum of eighteen thousand pictorial beatings, shootings, stranglings, blood-puddles, and torturings-to-death, from comic (ha-ha) books alone, identifying himself – unless he is a complete masochist – with the heroic beater, shooter, strangler, blood-letter, and/or torturer in every case. With repetition like that, you can teach a child anything: that black is white, to stand on his head, eat hair – anything. At the moment it is being used to teach him — and in no quiet professorial tone, but rather in flaming color and superheated dialogue — that violence is heroic, and murder a red-hot thrill.

The effect, if not the intention, has been to raise up an entire generation of adolescents — twenty million of them — who have felt, thousands upon thousands of times, all the sensations and emotions of committing murder, except pulling the trigger. And toy guns and fireworks, advertised in the back pages of the comics — cap-shooters, b-b rifles (with manufacturer's enscrolled Bill of Rights), paralysis pistols, crank'emup tommyguns, six-inch cannon-crackers, and ray-gats emitting a spark a foot and a half long — have supplied that. The Universal Military Training of the mind.

The theory on which we supply corpses to children, as playthings, is not a secret. If it is generally cloaked in the Aristotelian fustian of 'tragic catharsis,' and seldom put into plain words, it is because it does not make good listening. It is this: We train children as we train other animals, by breaking their spirit. We fit them, not for the life they are prepared for as they emerge from the womb — and no one has ever bothered to find out what that natural human life is — but rather for a very different civilized life, forced upon them ready-made by adults. The child's natural character — again, whatever it may be — must be distorted to fit civilization, just as his feet must be distorted to fit shoes. This is called education, and naturally the child resists it. But by feeding him blood he can be drugged into acquiescence while we break his spirit, distort his bones and his character, and, in a word, civilize him. Fantasy violence will paralyze his resistance, divert his aggression to unreal enemies and frustrations, and in this way prevent him from rebelling against parents & teachers busy abnormalizing him. When he grows up, the human sacrifices will be continued in all the popular arts with paid or accidental victims — as in prize-fights and headlines — and this will siphon off his resistance against society, and prevent revolution. At any rate, that is the theory. And if we accept the premise that the civilized life is better than the natural and worth distorting children to fit, there is no arguing with the methods that do the job. The method being blood, feed children blood.

Baldly stated — and I hope it is bald enough — that is the standard psychiatric justification for comic-books. Now let's examine it. Accept, for the moment, the premise that though we have more jails than we have high-schools, more insane-asylums than colleges, by some criterion our society can be called successful and ought to be kept going. But does the let-'em-eat-blood theory really work? Historically it has always failed. The gladiatorial arena did not save Rome. Instead, the breadmasters and slaves saw played before their eyes their own coming dissolution. The surfeit of death in the blood-drama of Marlowe and Shakespeare and Kyd did not avert the English Revolution. The Black Hundreds' butchering of Jews did not avert the Russian. The incinerating of six million more Jews in Germany did not preserve the Nazi régime. To the contrary, where institutionalized violence appears in history, it is as the last resort of bankrupt civilizations, sick and reeling into death.

The admission, so cheerfully made, that children *need* these aggressive outlets in fantasy against their parents, teachers, policemen, and total social environment is an admission that this social environment does not have a place for the child. The necessity for the same outlet by adults then means that the social environment has no place in it for adults. For whom has the social environment a place?

•

DISGUISES are still necessary. The public can hardly be told what is being done to it. And so, super-imposed on the pattern violence of its children's comics, there is a variety of titles, a variety of formulas suited to the age-groups and sexes the industry proposes to exploit: under six, six to ten, ten to fourteen, fourteen to sixteen, and up. The principal formulas, in the chronology of the age-groups they appeal to, are: the floppity-rabbit or kid comics, representing a tenth or less; the crime comics, one tenth last year, this year — having been legalized — a third or more; classical and educational, a tenth between them; Superman and his imitators, the most popular formula until the advent of crime, with about one third last year, this year a fifth; the squinkie or sex-horror group, another fifth; and the 'teenage or sex-hate group, a final fifth specifically for adolescent girls.

At the lowest age-level the necessary violence is presented as between little anthropomorphic animals — gouging, twisting, tearing, and mutilating one another (as will be seen) to a running accompaniment of all the loud noises and broad swift motions enjoyed by, and forbidden to, small children. The Katzenjammer pattern is abandoned. Menaces are created, because, against a menace, no extreme of brutality is forbidden, where, against Der Captain or Foxy Grandpa or 'Uncle' Donald Duck, nothing rougher than a pea-shooter and ridicule may be used. Also, and very importantly, where even the slightest overt hostility against these real parent-surrogates will inevitably be followed by punishment; no punishment at all, but rather rewards, will follow the total brutalization of a 'menace.'

In our culture the perversion of children has become an industry. When Mr. Walt Disney, the dean of that industry, sits down with his artists to put a nursery story into animated pictures, color, and sound, what do they do to it, to insure their investment of time & money? What did they do to *The Three Little Pigs,* their greatest triumph? They changed a story of diligence rewarded and laziness punished, into a Grand Guignol of wolf-tortured-by-pigs, complete with house-sized 'Wolf Pacifier' beating the wolf over the head with six rolling-pins, kicking him in the rump with as many automatic boots, and reserving bombs and TNT beneath, and a potty-chair overhead, to finish him off with. Pictures of this mechanism may be examined in Alfred H. Barr's *Fantastic Art* (1937) item 536.

The explanation — if anyone ever notices that an explanation is called for — is never, frankly, that the wolf is papa, tricked out in animal falseface so he can be righteously beaten to death. At most, one is privately given to understand that without this continual drug of violence, parents could not be protected from their children. The horse-dosage of sadism supplied for this purpose to nursery and crib, gives pause even to murder-movie director, John Houseman. Says Mr. Houseman — observing, naturally, the mote in his neighbor's eye to the exclusion of the beam in his own —

> I remember the time when Disney and his less successful imitators concerned themselves with the frolicsome habits of bees, birds, and the minor furry animals. *Joie-de-vivre* was the keynote. Sex and parenthood played an important and constructive rôle, illustrated by such cheerful fertility-symbols as storks, Easter eggs, bunnies, et cetera. Now all this is changed. The fantasies which our children greet with howls of joy run red with horrible savagery. Today the animated cartoon has become a bloody battlefield through which savage and remorseless creatures, with single-track minds, pursue one another, then rend, gouge, twist, tear, and mutilate each other with sadistic ferocity. ("What makes American movies tough?" *Vogue,* Jan. 15th, 1947 pages 88, 120.)

NOT FOR CHILDREN

One thing is certain: in our violent popular arts – and comic-books and Disney cartoons and Punch & Judy shows are only a few of them – children do not generally identify themselves with the victims of the violence. These are daydreams not nightmares. It is the child who is gloriously violent in these fantasies, as he dare not be in fact. And his victim is everyone else.

It was for lack of discernment on this point that critical surprise was expressed during the war – as by 'George Orwell' (Eric Blair) and the rest of the shabby-genteel school – when murder-mysteries for civilian consumption outsold all other pocket reprints into the hundred millions, while comic-books were the favorite, and practically the only, reading of the American soldier, outselling at PX's, by ten to one, *Life, Liberty, Reader's Digest,* and the *Saturday Evening Post* combined. It seemed odd that, after being exposed to violence and the fear of violence all day, soldiers and civilians should want to read about it all night. But the significant difference is again that in the violent fantasies of murder-mysteries and comic-books the reader is not being shot at – he does the shooting. He is no helpless victim, as he is in life. While he reads, he is the hero. While he reads, he is no well-bullied cog in the wheel – he is bigger than the wheel: he protects the wheel, and breaks it if he likes.

•

THE GLORIFICATION of crime is, by common consensus, unfit for children. That one third of all fiction printed, and two thirds of all comic-books, are nevertheless devoted to crime – specifically to the crime of murder – has been made possible by the Poe-èsque shifting of the accent, and the reader's identification-image, from the criminal to the avenger. The crime-content remains the same, even increases, since the reader no longer need have any sense of guilt in reading.

Until recently, fiction and comics simple-mindedly glorifying criminals instead of Supersleuths, or cowboy outlaws instead of G-men, had fallen upon lean days. Their formula was so closely watched, so loaded down with apologies and pious protestations of educational and didactic intent, that no one cared to read them. Hardly a tenth of all comic-books openly glorified crime, and even these had to take it all back in fatuous exhortations to law & order at the top of every page. It was also necessary, after every seven pages of glorious cop-killing and lawbreaking, to show the outlaw or gangster, at the bottom of page eight, full of bullet-holes and covered with blood. In other words, the Katzenjammer formula, but with killing instead of spanking as the punishment, since killing and not 'naughtiness' was the crime. This teaches the reader that *CRIME* – in big letters – and then in little letters underneath: *does not pay.* That's the title of the most successful crime-comic.

From 1937, when comic-books got under way, until the spring of 1948, when the United States Supreme Court struck down, in the Winters decision, all state laws against printed 'bloodshed, lust or crime' under which crime- and similar comics might have been suppressed (but never were), twenty crime-comics were being published. By the end of the year, one hundred new crime-comics opened shop – first gangster, then cowboy when the publishers' nerve failed – with no similar increase in any other type. *GANGSTERS – can't win. LAWBREAKERS – always lose. CRIME – and punishment. CRIMINALS – on the run* (formerly *Young King Cole*). *GUNS – of fact and fiction* (formerly *A-1*). Or the apologetics can come first, in the usual small type, and the selling plug last: *Justice traps the GUILTY, Crime must pay the PENALTY, There is no escape for PUBLIC ENEMIES,* or, as the final bathetic convolution of a publisher's bad conscience (the distributors have none), *Hard-hitting agents of the law strike at the . . . UNDERWORLD,* with a cover-illustration showing a criminal slapping a woman in the face. And ninety-odd more.

The manufacturers are not as proud of their new abundance as they might be, disguising the first issue of their two new crime-kicks a week as #3 (*Saddle Justice*), #33 (*Crime must pay the PENALTY*), and #103 (*All-American Western*), but the total is not hard to cast. In ten years, twenty. In one year, a hundred. When the highest court in the land protects it, crime pays.

●

LIKE THE toy gun and cowboy suit that are its concomitants, the crime-comic is for the younger child. When children get to be nine or ten, and parents begin to realize that thumbing through little pictures of talking animals massacring one another can hardly be called literate, while similar massacres as between cops & robbers can hardly

NOT FOR CHILDREN

be called constructive, the necessary violence gets a quick coat of literary paint by the industry, and re-appears under the respectable camouflage of being 'classic.' What is meant by 'classic' is that all the most violent children's books of the last two centuries are condensed into forty-eight-page picture-sequences, omitting every literary element but the rougher dialogue, and stringing and squeezing together into four dozen pages every violent scene that can be found anywhere in the three hundred or more text-pages of the original 'classic.' Dickens becomes a library of terror. Dumas, Cooper, Stevenson, and Scott – massacres complete. And if the chosen 'classic' should happen to run short on violence, extra violence can always be added, as in the *Three Little Pigs*.

After being processed in this way, no classic, no matter who wrote it, is in any way distinguishable from the floppity-rabbit and crime comics it is supposed to replace, except that it has a sort of seal of approval: it's been printed in 'hard-cover' books – as they're called by people who do not read them – and so it must be all right. As the final meretricious touch to the disguise, one sequence in every 'classic' comic must always be some tender little sob-story like *Laddie* or *Black Beauty*, teaching that we should all be kind to dumb animals. This not only adds an elevating flavor of humanitarianism to the whole enterprise, but also helps the reader to graduate, at the age of ten, from animal victims to human.

Parent-Teacher associations assemble. They are worried – not by the violence in comic-books: they approve of that. They are worried by the exclusive absorption with which the children lap it up. Their education is being neglected, the very education that this mad-dog biscuit of violence was supposed to protect. And the manufacturers are spurred to action. They hire child-psychologists, educators, clergymen, quiz-kids, criminologists, public-opinion pollsters; and under their supervision the comics become 'educational,' meaning that instead of fictional violence, factual violence will be substituted.

History and biography are ransacked. Science is turned upside down. Every war since Cain & Abel's is retold in the usual fifty little pictures as one continuous jamboree of corpses. The Indians are killed off twice a week, and, when they are gone, outlaws and sheriffs battle it out with six-guns for the American dirt the Indians no longer need. Alfred Nobel is made educational in eight pages of dynamite explosions, Florence Nightingale in eight pages of Crimean war horror. Teddy Roosevelt, eight pages of buffalo-killing and boxing gloves. Louis Pasteur — this was a hard one — eight pages of corpuscles killing germs. This is 'educational.' There are even Bible comics: eight pages of Jesus Christ flagellated, on the cross, dripping blood. Why not? It's not only classic, it's sacred; it can be enjoyed on the walls of any Catholic church. And for the cover-illustration: David cutting off Goliath's head with a bloody sword. The more famous part of that particular story is that David hit him with a slingshot, but a sword and blood and a severed head are more 'educational.'

It is hard to believe that the child-psychologists and educators who accept fees for signing their names to the mast-heads of 'classic' and 'educational' comics are really so naïve as not to realize that the products they are fronting for are immeasurably more harmful than the crime-comics they intend to replace (when they do not turn into them, as in *Parents' Magazine's* FBI and 'Fighting Frontier Sheriff' comics, formerly *True* and *Calling All Boys*). Hypocritically or not, the crime-comic does tell the child that murder is the act of a criminal, and will be punished. The educational comic tells him the opposite. It gives murder prestige. It *sells* children on murder the way tooth-paste is sold. Movie stars do it, duchesses do it, men of distinction do it — why don't you? The educational comic glorifies murder, as the crime-comic cannot, with all the prestige of science, classics, the Bible, patriotism, *Geheimpolizei,* and every other possible incentive to emulation. Captain Eddie Rickenbacker killed so many and so many men. Go thou and do thou likewise. Not only murder is no longer a crime, and need not be punished; in the educational comic, murder is rewarded. Murder is heroic.

•

IT IS THIS same ability to transcend all human law, and be honored for it instead of punished, that makes the Superman formula so successful. Crime comics are generally frowned upon because of the obvious insincerity of their last-page exhortations to law & order. And so, Superman reverses the formula. He takes the crime for granted, and then spends thirty pages violently avenging it. He can fly, he can see through brick walls, he can stop the sun in its orbit like a second Joshua; and all this godlike power he focuses on some two-bit criminal or crackpot, who hasn't even pulled a trigger yet but is only threatening to. Giant the Jack-killer. And of course, all of Superman's violence being on the side of right, there is no necessity

NOT FOR CHILDREN

for any Katzenjammer-Kid punishment on the last page. If Superman is punished at all, his punishment is something like Blondie's: implicit in his status, in the fact that he is really only an unvirile clerk who wears glasses and can't get the girl – like the reader. And this obvious flimflam suffices to blind parents & teachers to the glaring fact that not only Superman, and his even more violent imitators, invest violence with righteousness and prestige – something that the crime-comics can never do, and that the 'educationals' can only hope to, since children will not read them – but that the Superman formula is essentially lynching.

In the hands of the Supermen, private justice takes over. Legal process is completely discounted and contemptuously by-passed. No trial is necessary, no stupid policemen hog all the fun. Fists crashing into faces become the court of highest appeal. And if Superman himself does not shed blood, few of his imitators are quite so careful. The question is not whether Superman flies because children object to the law of gravity, or because the flying dream is a disguised and therefore allowable eroticism. (Sigmund Freud: *Die Traumdeutung*. 1900, chapter 5, D-*b*-IV.) The question is: what has become of the law & order that all the Supermen are supposedly upholding?

After six thousand pictures (per child) of these super-flying, -swimming, -bouncing, -jumping, and otherwise contra-gravitationally progressing gazeebos taking the law into their own hands for its own good – the black mask constant among all their copyrightable peculiarities – of what, precisely, has the reader been convinced by Aquaman, Batman, Blackhawk, Black Hood, Black Knight, Blackstone, Black Terror (his insignia a skull & crossbones), Black X, Blue Beetle (a policeman in his spare time), Boy Commandos, Captain America, Captains Marvel and Marvel Jr., Captain Midnight, Captain Triumph, Catman & Kitten (a girl-helper for a change); Doc Strange, Doll Man, Dr. Mid-nite, Dynamic Man, Fighting Yank, Funnyman (Superman's second-string imbecility), Golden Archer, Golden Arrow, Golden Lad, Green Hornet, Green Lantern & Doiby, Green Mantle, Human Torch & Toro, Ibis the Invisible, The Jester (another policeman), Kid Eternity, Mad Hatter, Magno & Davey, Manhunter & his faithful dog Thor (still another policeman. but 'police are limited'), Marvel Man & Vana, Master Key, Minute Man, Mr. Scarlet & Pinky (goak), Phantasmo, Phantom Eagle & Commando Yank, Plastic Man, Professor Supermind & Son – not getting bored, are you? the kids eat this up by the thousand ton –

LOVE & DEATH

Pyroman, The Reckoner & Chipper; Red, White & Blue, Rocket Man, The Scarab, Silver Streak, Skyman, Spirit of '76 & Tubby, Star Pirate, Sub-mariner, Superboy ('Crime-fighting Poet'), Superman, Super Rabbit, Supersnipe, Target & the Targeteers, Yankee Boy, Yankee Doodle Jones & Dandy (who gets his strength from a hypodermic needle), and Wonderman. An abbreviated list, of course.

The truth is that the Superman formula is, in every particular, the exact opposite of what it pretends to be. Instead of teaching obedience to law, Superman glorifies the 'right' of the individual to take that law into his own hands. Instead of preaching the 100% Americanism that he and his cruder imitators express in hangmen's suits of red-white-&-blue, Superman – as Sterling North long ago pointed out (Chicago *Daily News,* May 8th, 1940) – is really peddling a philosophy of 'hooded justice' in no way distinguishable from that of Hitler and the Ku Klux Klan. Instead of being a gallant hangover from the feudal knighthood of *combat seul* – the sort of thing aviators like to play at – Superman is actually not above accompanying his endless rights to the jaw with snide wisecracks like 'I do wish you fellows would listen to reason,' or 'Ho hum, here we go again.'

Most significant of all, instead of being brave and fearless, Superman lives really in a continuous guilty terror, projecting outward in every direction his readers' paranoid hostility. Every city in America is in the grip of fiends. Every mayor, governor, senator, president – even a district attorney or two – is totally corrupt and/or in cahoots with spies. Every country in the world is about to attack us – with our own bombs. Mars is almost ready to blow us out of the cosmos – with our own rockets. And of course the army, the navy, the police and the FBI, and all the resources of civilization are powerless. Only the Nazi-Nietzschean *Übermensch,* in his provincial apotheosis as Superman, can save us.

> The constant traffic with the world of crime [says Walter J. Ong], provides a suitable culture for the paranoic patriotism . . . found festering at the roots of recent Germany . . . "Clark Kent," Superman is told, "you're a pessimist! To listen to you, anyone would think this town was full of crooks!" The guardian of American ideals glances casually over his shoulder. Crooks everywhere. It is not far to go from this world of total crime to the persecution complex of the neurotic. (*Arizona Quarterly,* Autumn 1945, page 41.)

NOT FOR CHILDREN

AMERICANS are the only modern people (except the Boers) who, within living memory, have killed off the original population of the country in which they live. Only in America, therefore, has a national bad conscience had to be stilled by inventing the type-myth of the 'bad Injun' to replace the plain historical fact of an honorable Redskin unsuccessfully defending his land from gun- and Bible-bearing invaders. Our merited punishment can be averted only by denying that evil has been done, by throwing the blame upon the victim, by proving – to our own satisfaction at least – that in striking the first and only blow we were acting simply in self-defense . . . as against the Indians, who owned this country before we got here, and are now nowhere to be seen.

Stunned by our own guilt – as now again with the atom-bomb – we find ourselves desperate either to fasten this guilt upon someone else, or to confuse our fear of punishment with the disproportionate aggression against which we struck. The daily conviction that we are menaced in our innocence, and not by our guilt, must at all costs be maintained. Our mental 'preparedness' must be kept at the exploding point, looking always outward and never in. When bad Injuns run short, the ubiquitous rustler is raised up to replace them. When both disappear, and the gangster along with them, it becomes necessary to go shopping for victims. Whole literatures produce fantasy scapegoats for us to murder by the bookful – flogging-blocks, daily to pummel and destroy – all leering horribly, as per contract, in synthetic menace.

It was in conformity with this pattern that Americans leapt into the street with shotguns and brickbats when, on Hallowe'en 1938, on the eve of war, the radio assured them that octopedal Martians had landed in Sleepyville, New Jersey. It would have been inconceivable – as much to Ringmasters H. G. and Orson Welles as to the public – that the Martians might come with the outstretched tentacle of friendship, eager to exchange folk-dances and encyclopedias. No. If we went to Mars – yes, and if we *do* go to Mars – it will be with the naked sword, the cocked gun, the long-nosed bomber (with the motor behind), or with whatever the current camouflage-symbol for aggressive virility with the prepuce retracted may be. To excuse ourselves in advance, we have merely to project our intended aggression upon our intended victim.

Into this well-manured soil of national guilt, fear, and renewed aggression – in ascending spirals – the Superman virus was sown.

LOVE & DEATH

Not, of course, by the two nice Jewish boys who take the credit, Messrs. Shuster and Siegel, but by Hitler. With only this difference that, in the ten-year effort to keep supplying sinister victims for the Supermen to destroy, comic-books have succeeded in giving every American child a complete course in paranoid megalomania such as no German child ever had, a total conviction of the morality of force such as no Nazi could even aspire to.

Nor are the comic-books lacking in any of the trappings of their Naziism. It may even be that they are not unconscious of their function as pilot-plants for the fascist state. There is the same appeal to pagan gods for totally unearned powers – Wodin, Thoth, Oom, Ug, and the rest of that pantheon. There is the same exploitation of magical insignia: Superman's big 'S' without which he is powerless, The Flash's thunderbolt, also Captain Marvel's – a swastika is two thunderbolts crossing, one on the sleeve as the *Turnverein* symbol, the other in the pocket waiting for *der Tag* – the Lone Ranger's even clearer monogram, lacking only one leg of being a swastika complete.

There is the same needful creation of a super-menace to excuse the creation of the super-avenger. There is the same anti-intellectuality, not only in the worship of 'coat-hanger shoulders and nutcracker jaws' (Marya Mannes, in *Town Meeting of the Air*, March 2nd, 1948, page 9), and in the stock character of the 'mad' scientist, but in actual propaganda strips showing whole hordes of scientists in white coats setting out to enslave and destroy the world. When the comic-book reader hears the word 'culture,' he too reaches for the safety-catch of his revolver. There is of course the same anti-Semitism: *all* the more sinister villians have 'Jewish' noses. In some cases the hook-nose is the only way to tell the equally bloodthirsty villain and (snub-nosed) hero apart. There is the same glorification of uniforms, riding boots, and crushed caps: Blackhawk, for instance, and his international lynch mob, are dressed from tip to toe in the Gestapo uniform, but in state-trooper blue instead of black. And there is the same undercurrent of homosexuality and sado-masochism.

The exploitation of brutality and terror is blatantly apparent. The homosexual element lies somewhat deeper. It is not – at least, not importantly – in the obvious faggotry of men kissing one another and saying 'I love you,' and then flying off through space against orgasm backgrounds of red and purple, not in the transvestist scenes in every kind of comic-book from floppity-rabbits to horror-squinkies, not in the long-haired western killers with tight pants (for choice). Neither is it in the explicit Samurai subservience of the inevitable little-boy helpers – theoretically identification shoe-horns for children not quite bold enough to identify themselves with Superprig himself – nor in the fainting adulation of thick necks, ham fists, and well-filled jockstraps; the draggy capes and costumes, the shamanistic talismans and superstitions that turn a sissified clerk into a one-man flying lynch-mob with biceps bigger than his brain. It is not even in the two comic-book companies staffed entirely by homosexuals and operating out of our most phalliform skyscraper.

The really important homosexuality of the Superman theme – as deep in the hub of the formula as the clothes and kisses are at the periphery – is in the lynching pattern itself, in the weak and fearful righteousness with which it achieves its wrong. No matter how bad criminals (or even crime-comics) may be, in identifying himself with them the child does consummate his Oedipean dream of strength: the criminal does break through his environment. The Supermen, the Supersleuths, the Supercops do not. They align themselves always on the side of law, authority, the father; and accept their power passively from a bearded above. They are not competing – not for the forbidden mother, not for any other reward. Like Wild Bill Hickok, our own homosexual hero out thar where men were men – with his long silk stockings and his Lesbian side-kick, Calamity Jane – they are too unvirile to throw off fear, and kill as criminals. Instead, unseen and unsuspected in some corner, they put on a black mask, a sheriff's badge and a Superman suit, and do all their killing on the side of the law.

•

THE FIRST argument invariably brought forward when anyone wants to suppress a book, is 'What might it do to innocent children?' This attempted moronization of all art, scaling it down to the point where it will not excite to masturbation even the most willing child, has of course, a certain logic in a culture where the average mental age is fourteen. I do not intend to pursue this argument here, nor to study its clear, though frustrated, pedophilia. (A good beginning for such a study might be Anthony Comstock's 'wooden snake' that he 'carried in his pocket' and 'produced upon occasion to frighten a girl whom he used to visit.' – Heywood Broun: *Anthony Comstock, Roundsman of the Lord*, 1927, page 12.) I prefer, rather, to examine just what we do give our five-, six-, and ten-year-old children;

just what, apparently does fit their needs and their innocence, as *Lady Chatterley's Lover* would not.

It is the intention of the comic-book industry and its bought psychologists, to focus the attack on comic-books, now gathering, against the sexual element in them – against the normal sexual element. Emotionalized words like 'pornography' and so on, are carefully bandied about. Mr. George Hecht of *Parents' Magazine,* whose comics publish only the 'educational' brand of violence, draws up and circulates a sex-censorship code for comic-books (New York *Times,* July 2nd, 1948, page 23, with no mention of Mr. Hecht, whose original eleven points – six anti-sexual – are here cut down to half.) Nor is it hard to see what the plan is.

If public resistance to comic-books becomes sufficiently articulate – and the results of one public-opinion poll have already been suppressed – the attack is to be diverted into a big clean-up drive against the so-called sex-horror or squinkie comics, representing no more than one fifth of the total. When the clamor dies down, the other four fifths will still be in business peddling the same old violence, the same old illiteracy, the same old 'passive reception of manufactured entertainment,' requiring of the reader nothing more than to hand over his ten cents and then sit there drugged while little effortless pictures flow over him, isolate him in a world of suspicion and fear, and leave him mentally helpless and still frustrated, floundering in imaginary blood.

As to the accusation that certain comic-books might excite young children sexually – and that this would be wrong – one can only assume that Mr. Hecht and the other would-be sex-censors of comics imagine that what excites them will also excite children. Actually, they have not the slightest recollection of what does excite young children sexually. Here is part of Dr. Glenn Ramsey's list of what *did* excite 291 younger boys:

> Being scared, Fear of a house intruder, Near accidents . . . Seeing a policeman, Cops chasing him . . . Big fires, Setting a field afire, Hearing a revolver shot, Anger, Watching exciting games, Playing in exciting games, Marching soldiers, War motion pictures . . . Band music, Hearing "extra paper" called, Harsh words, Fear of punishment, Being yelled at, Being alone at night, Fear of a big boy . . . Losing balance on heights, Looking over edge of building, Falling from garage,

NOT FOR CHILDREN

Long flight of stairs, Adventure stories, National anthem, Watching a stunting airplane, Finding money ... Detective stories, Running away from home, Entering an empty house, Nocturnal dreams of fighting, accidents, wild animals, falling from high places, giants, being chased, or frightened. (*American Journal of Psychology*, 1943, vol. 56: pages 222-223; revised in Alfred C. Kinsey &c. *Sexual Behavior in the Human Male*, 1948, pages 164-165.)

If it is really the intention to censor comic-books of everything – not that might, but that does excite children sexually, that list should put them all out of business. Possibly for this reason, the sexuality of comic-books is discovered, not in their stupendous dosage of sado-masochistic excitements, but in the female breast. What the complaint generally boils down to is that the women in certain comic-books have highly developed binocular bosoms, and run around in brassière & panties. Armpit-hair is also sometimes suggested. As the British critics observed concerning *The Outlaw*, just what there is about a woman's *un*-brassiered breasts that would come as a surprise to even a nursing child is hard to say. But the really surprising thing is the hypocrisy that can examine all these thousands of pictures in comic-books showing half-naked women being tortured to death, and complain only that they're half naked. If they were being tortured to death with all their clothes on, that would be perfect for children.

Now, what is it that is supposed to be attractive to 12- and 14-year-old boys about torturing women to death, with or without their clothes, about tying them up with ropes and chains, whipping them, branding them on the modestly un-nippled breast, skewering their throats with javelins, pumping their veins empty (or full of unheard-of viruses), throwing them to wild animals, shooting them in the belly with hot lead? What is it that makes adolescents buy eight million dollars' worth of comic-books yearly in which those are the principal themes both outside and in? That the publishers, editors, artists, and writers of comic-books are degenerates and belong in jail, goes without saying; but what makes millions of adolescents willing to accept degeneracy too? It can hardly be the transparent squinkie disguise: that the woman is being tortured so the hero can rescue her. As far as the publishers are concerned, the explanation is simply that that is the way our censorship works. The sadism in comics is substituted for sex. Under American law — now brass-bound in a Supreme Court decision — sex in literature is worse than murder. The publisher of a novel in which intercourse is described goes to jail. The publishers of pocket reprints — seventy or more percent murder — make a million dollars.

Comic-book publishers, and the very respectable magazine distributors anonymous behind them, are after that million dollars too. This is not to suggest that any one or any group sits wilily down to say, '*Hovo nis-hockmo lo* — come, let us deal wisely with them — let us pervert the children of a nation for a penny apiece. Let us stupefy their minds. Let us inflame their imaginations with violence and death. Let us deliver them over to the pleasures of sadist-masturbation for that all-mighty penny apiece.' Nobody says it that way. They conjure instead with the heap big magic of 'Business is business,' of 'If we don't do it someone else will' (the naked backside of the Christian ethic), of '*Who* can make money educating the public?'

Mr. Coulton Waugh, in the sixteenth and final chapters of his recent history of *The Comics* (1947), has given a punctilious accounting of every hard-faced little businessman — even the binder — who had a finger in the baking of the fifty-million-dollar comic-book pie. To Mr. Waugh the comic-book is a thunderclap. He sees it gathering like a golden cloud, ready to rain down into the Danaëan lap of the Eastern Color Printing Company. He sees nothing of the erotic comic-books, imported from Cuba and Mexico, and published surreptitiously here, since the mid-1920's, with daily comic-strip characters in sexual scenes: Maggie & Jiggs, Tillie & Mac —'Sent In Plain Wrapper . . . Kind Men Like' — America's only original contribution to the development of the comics. Mr. Waugh sees nothing significant in the background shift from sex to violence common to the biggest-shots of the comics industry today — the *Whiz Bang* Fawcetts, the *Snappy Stories* (now *Superman*) Donenfelds, &c. — and therefore fails to observe that the total achievement of all these gentlemen of vision was nothing more than to substitute legal blood for illegal semen, crime for coitus, in the erotic comic-book of a dozen years' standing, quadrupling its size fearlessly as they brought it forth from under the counter, legal now in its sadism where it had been criminal then in its sex.

With the passing of the word 'sadism' into the English language, the essential fact of its *perversion* — its repression and redirection of normal sexual impulses — has been carefully lost sight of. Even where this basic substitution between the two is recognized, the direction of the exchange is preposterously reversed, and we are asked to believe that sadism is the normal emotional state in children, and is transformed – or should one say perverted? – into sexuality in grown-ups.

Children, we are told – and told it often – are naturally cruel. They tear the wings off flies. So they do. Children are also naturally sexual. They examine each other's genitals, and masturbate. Why is this worse? Why is sadism in children 'innocuous ferocity' while masturbation is a sin & a shame? But that is the double standard whereby we manipulate children. The preference for sadism over sex is not any child's free choice. The substitution of an allowed pathology for a censored normality is not the spontaneous activity of 'naturally cruel' child minds. It is specifically a diversion required of children – in the case of the comics, created for them – by adults.

There, in the censoring of normality into pathology, is your million dollars. The comic-book publishers capitalize on the ease with which the nascent and frustrated sexuality of adolescents can be perverted. It cannot seriously be held that 12- and 14-year-old boys have sexual impulses sufficiently developed to require siphoning off into a sadism of quite the incredible dimensions of the comic books'. But a pattern is formed. The comic-books show the woman half-naked. They lay her down on the sacrificial altar. They spread one leg here and one leg there – and then they beat her to death. If there can be any question that this is an aborted sexual act, I don't know in whose mind. Nevertheless, it gets by the censorship – both the legal censorship and the internalized censorship of the unconscious mind – because what looks as though it's going to end in sexual intercourse merely ends in death.

Naturally, this formula is not popular with girls. Granting all the masochistic excitement of terror, it is difficult to identify yourself with a corpse. And so there are published not only a handful of female crime- and western-comics, but whole series of so-called 'teenage comic-books specifically for girls, in which adolescent sexuality is achieved in sadistic disguise, without father-daughter incest, without intercourse, without petting, without even a single kiss, through a continuous humiliation of scarecrow fathers and transvestist boyfriends by ravishingly pretty girls, beating up the men with flowerpots and clocks and brooms, wearing their clothes, throwing them out of windows, setting them on fire, pulling out their teeth with pliers, smashing them in the face with flatirons, and breaking bottles of ketchup over their heads so as not to deprive young readers of the sight of something that at least *looks* like blood. (With the exception of the standard ketchup-trick, all these are from a single 'teen age comic, *Jeanie* #16.)

There is even a 'comic' super-female (with the usual imitators), Wonder Woman: strictly *Weiberherrschaft*, strictly Lesbianism, strictly female domination of the male, originated by a self-confessed masochist, Professor William Moulton Marston, who explains:

> Men actually submit to women now, they do it on the sly with a sheepish grin because they're ashamed of being ruled by weaklings. Give them an alluring woman stronger than themselves to submit to and they'll be *proud* to become her willing slaves. (*Time*, October 22nd, 1945, page 68.)

Wonder Woman's 'allure' is, of course, sexless, synthetic – the drum-majorette patriotism of star-spangled panties and spread-eagled breasts. On her own time she is straight *Wunschprojektion* for the envious female – Blondie with a bull-whip, an Amazon with mannish coat & tie and the curtly chaste cognomen of 'Diana Prince.'

Dr. Lauretta Bender, chief pot-washer and apologist for the comics industry, goes Dr. Marston one better, calling this obvious unsexing and perversion 'A strikingly advanced concept of femininity and masculinity' (*American Journal of Orthopsychiatry*, 1941, vol. 11: page 547), and, in accordance with it, the Superman theme and all its symbols are reversed. Where the Supermen have ridiculously over-inflated genitals – never mentioned in objecting to the women's breasts – Wonder Woman has her yonijic lariat with a loop a yard and a half across. That is her trade-mark (her imitators all have something similar), and by its means she lynches her spate of criminals, and humiliates and big-sisters all the other males in the strip.

As to this enormous use of sexual symbols in comic-books it is almost useless to speak, except to mention that it is a predictable enough result of censorship: the whales rushing up between the legs of women who go out to fish for minnows (*Jumbo Comics* #94), the rhinoceros with double horns on his nose coming up at a six-year-old girl-child in the crotch (*Fight Comics* #48), the moon-rockets with the red tips to which interplanetary women-captives must be bound (this is standard), the snakes, the whips, the endless revolvers and automatics aimed from and at the groin, if not at the buttocks;

NOT FOR CHILDREN

and, at the absolute nadir of indefensible vulgarity, the habitual desecration of women in wedding gowns, now repeated on the cover of *Claire Voyant Comics* #3, reprinted from the newspaper *PM* where the bride is socked on the chin with the butt of a gun, thrown in the mud in her white tulle gown, and finally picked up by a Lesbian driving a truck marked FISH in letters apparently two feet high.

•

GO BACK NOW to the standard psychiatric justification, that violence in fantasy will prevent violence in fact, that perversion on paper is social therapy, and ask whether any such social benefits can be shown to have accrued in these ten years of comic-books. Never before in the history of the world has a literature like this, specifically for children, ever existed — certainly not in the pink blood & tinpot thunder of your grandfather's yellowback, not in the illustrated martyrologies of Gallonio and Foxe at their grisliest, not in the macabré Dances of Death of another expiring dark age. (Johan Huizinga: *The Waning of the Middle Ages*, 1924, chapter 11, "The Vision of Death.") Where is the promised prevention of violence supposed to result from all this flagellation and blood, all this killing, all these dying grunts and gasps, these punched out teeth, chopped off hands, and twisted off heads, these hypodermic needles jabbed into eyes (reproduced by Dr. Fredric Wertham in *Saturday Review of Literature*, May 29th, 1948, page 7), these women branded on the breast with red-hot snake-shaped irons, this insane metronomic repetition of 'the human fist hitting the human face' (Marya Mannes, in *New Republic*, February 17th, 1947, page 23). Just ask. The publishers prefer not to answer. They have the unparalleled gall to demand that the opponents of comic-books prove instead that harm has been done.

Of course, if they were still publishing erotic comics, no such proof would be necessary. The mere possibility of 'harm' would be enough to jail them. But murder is different. No matter how many children commit killings exactly imitated from comic-books, and produce the comics to prove it, psychiatrists and educators can always be found to say that the child was neurotic in the first place. You bet your boots he was! After eighteen thousand little pictures of ecstatic murder and heroic sadism, who wouldn't be? But the more serious charge, the provable charge, that twenty million children have been brought up on violence, and sleep it, and eat it, and dream it,

LOVE & DEATH

and love it to the marrow of their bones – and therefore can never love anything or anyone else – that goes by the board.

People want to know what can be done. Nothing can be done. Not for children. Comic-books do not exist in a vacuum. American parents see nothing wrong with the fictional violence of comic-books because they are themselves addicted to precisely the same violence in reality, from the daily accident or atrocity smeared over the front page of their breakfast newspaper to the nightly prize-fight or murder-play in movies, radio, and television coast-to-coast.

It is necessary to be realistic. Violence in America is a business – big business – and everybody is in it, either as peddler or customer. It is one thing to attack a fifty-million-dollar racket perverting children. It is another thing to indict a five-hundred-million dollar industry pandering sadism to thoroughly perverted adults. Forget, for the moment, about comic-books. What about murder-mysteries? What about the pulps? What about newspapers, picture-mags, movies, radio, television – all plugging away as hard as ever they can on the same bloody one-note, while a civilization lathers itself up for murder.

Why just the comics? Is anyone trying to outlaw murder-mysteries, rented out at a dime a day, sold outright in pocket reprints and detective slicks for a quarter – one third of all fiction printed in English, the largest single segment of literature on earth? Are new laws passed to stop up this broken dam of literary bloodlust, the floodgates unscrewed and the handle thrown away by the Supreme Court?

At the lowest, broadest level, is anyone interested in outlawing pulp – the sole reading, with the newspaper, of tens of millions at the threshold of literacy – half of it straight murder, the other half divided up among an 'action' group that is mostly murder too: cowboy, northwest, aviation, jungle, pirate, 'sports,' supernatural, and fantasy-future, the last a typical paranoid rewriting of earth-attacking 'blue gloops and green bloops in . . . interplanetary cowboy yarns' (Phil Stong: *The Other Worlds*, 1941, page 16). There used to be a group of 'spicy' and 'snappy' sex-pulps to match, but the Post-Office stopped them. The love-by-the-rubber-plant pulps and the 'confession' slicks that women read, is anyone trying to stop *them*, with their simple translation of this drone-bass of violence into terms suitable for the female trade: illegitimate babies, humiliated mistresses, deserted wives, beaten brides, lives of shame, &c. – crucifying their paper-puppet heroines monthly on Richardson and Walpole's changeless principle: 'Make her suffer!'

NOT FOR CHILDREN

Does anyone find anything unwholesome in radio 'entertainment' — the soap-, crime-, and horse-operas — goosing Gothic masochism into mama in the morning (or she cannot work), titillating frustrated papa with horror until midnight (or he cannot sleep), dinning lynch-law into little Junior before supper (or he will not eat). Perversion as incentive, soporific, digestive! When radio broadcasters announce — and in an advertisement unmatched in its jovial gruesomeness since the fifteenth century (*New Yorker,* January 3rd, 1948, pages 12-13) — that murder-programs will no longer be broadcast earlier than 9:30 p.m., New York time, when all good children are asleep, does Los Angeles protest that this is only 6:30, Denver only 7:30, Chicago only 8:30 there?

Does anyone notice that in radio & television we now see happening what was sworn never would happen: fantasy bloodlust spilling over into fact, with prize-fights, wrestling matches, football and ice-hockey — once rough competitions, now holocausts of berserk bone-crushing while televised millions wet their pants — authors thrown to critics, contests in abuse and blatherskite under the name of comedy, spot-news broadcasts from the foot of the electric chair, paid sadistic quizmasters cracking the whip over fumbling quizzees, their trash-filled brains reeling between avarice and insult, audience-humiliation programs (under the guise of confessionals and giveaways) capitalizing on mayhem and sado-masochism in the nth degree, with the payoff to the victims in refrigerators?

Does anyone see anything hypocritical in 'tough'-movie director Houseman complaining about the violence of animated cartoons, in comics-artist 'Available' Al Capp replying for the industry that Shakespeare is 'full of murder . . . and S-E-X, too' (*Town Meeting of the Air,* March 2nd, 1948, page 12), in the spectacle of Los Angeles taking time off from its principal industry, the shipping out of psycho-thrillers and murder-movies hourly in cans, to observe that it is not amused by the 'funnies' (AP dispatch, September 22nd) and to pass a now-unconstitutional ordinance against them — anything ridiculous at all in these muck-filled pots calling the kettle black-ass?

Does anyone observe that the Catholic movie censorship and its Breen office, that so successfully prevented movie audiences from seeing — not the breasts, but the groove between the breasts of Miss Jane Russell in *The Outlaw,* has no objection to the glorification of Billy the Kid, the outlaw referred to, and a dozen others; no objec-

51

LOVE & DEATH

tion to Hollywood's New Violence that has shocked the world as ill becoming the nation that killed the most and lost the least in the recent war, no objection whatever to movie after movie called things like *Brute Force, The Killers, Ruthless, Relentless, Whiplash, Raw Deal, Coroner's Creek* (with blood and smashed bodies in full tomato-red; these and eighty like them, the product of a single year), wallowing in murder on both sides of the law, even in Loeb & Leopold's lust-murder in Mr. Alfred Hitchc—k's *Rope;* movie after movie in which a Hollywood homosexual in a three-day growth of beard smashes a woman in the face with half a cantaloupe or a flaming omelette (this is the well-known sanctity of the home, or *casti connubii,* that the censorship is intended to protect), movie after movie brutal and intended to brutalize, criminal by choice, perverse in every implication, and advertised as having, and I quote, 'all the impact of a slug in the guts'? The parallel development in the German movie, and where it led, is written plainly on the wall in Siegfried Kracauer's *From Caligari to Hitler* (1947) chapter 18, "Murderer Among Us" – though no German movie was ever advertised with billboards plastered across-country saying 'See a man pummelled to death with bare fists . . . See a man burned alive by steam.' But the working abridgment of the movie censorship code of the Reverend Martin Lord, S. J. has been adhered to: 'No tits – blood!' And there is no complaint.

Does anyone object, *ex cathedra,* that great religious enterprises like *Life* magazine (anatomized down to the last knuckle by Herbert M. McLuhan in *View,* Spring 1947) do not have to specialize in pictures of disembowelled corpses – with, of course, a handkerchief draped carefully over the penis, as on the Cross. Or, not to mention 'Weegee' and the New York *Daily Mirror,* glorying in their pictorial sadism – 'stark, graphic, exclusive' – and presenting portfolios of it to favored friends (*Camera Cavalcade,* 1946), does anyone go so far as to suggest that great liberal tabloids like *PM* do not really have to run Christmas close-ups of women suicides on their front pages with the caption, and again I quote, 'Ten seconds later she was dead' (December 23rd, 1947). You will notice that they did not run a picture of Princess Elizabeth's wedding with the caption 'Ten seconds later she was ─── ' There seems to be a word missing here. That's how it works. Death, yes. Sex, no.

Again, it is necessary to be realistic. Our civilization is not ready to let love and death fight it out in the market-place, with free speech

NOT FOR CHILDREN

and four-color printing on both sides. Our censors — private and public — are not ready to see, in their total concentration on 'impurity,' the breach through which this backwash of unimaginable violence rolls over us. Our publishers are not ready to stop telling writers — as they have told me — 'Any lousy, rotten thing you want to put on paper is O.K. with the district attorney, but if you put into a novel the description of the ordinary act of sexual intercourse between a man and wife, we will go to jail.'

The defenders of free speech generally break down at about that point, too. They are all willing to take the chance that murder-comics, murder-magazines, murder-headlines, murder-books, murder-movies, murder-ra'o & television — strange how respectable all these are, when 'sex book' is a sneer — murder, murder, murder, murder, a steady total dose of murder, will not harm in the slightest degree the most impressionable child or adult. But no one seems willing to suggest that in that case the plainest pornography would hurt them even less. At least sex is normal. Is murder?

It is an open question whether the maniacal fixation on violence and death in all our mass-produced fantasies is a substitution for a censored sexuality, or is, to a greater degree, intended to siphon off — into avenues of perversion opened up by the censorship of sex — the aggression felt by children and adults against the social & economic structure by which and to which they allow themselves to be distorted. In either case the distorting element is basic, whether sexual or economic, and until we are prepared to come to grips with these basic repressions, any attack on mere escape-mechanisms like comic-books must be futile.

•

CRIME COMICS, 1937-1947

All-True Crime	Official True Crime	Suspense
CRIME — does not pay	Police	Wanted
Detective	Real Clue Crime	
Dynamic	Real Fact	
Headline	The Shadow	Cow Puncher
Justice	The Spirit	Red Ryder
Kerry Drake Detective	Super-Mystery	The Westerner

NEW CRIME COMICS, 1948

Almanac of Crime (25c)
Authentic Police Cases
Blue Beetle (*new policy*)
Charlie Chan
Claire Voyant
Complete Mystery
CRIME – and punishment
Crime Detective
Crime Exposed
CRIMEfighters –
   always win
Crime Patrol
Crime Reporter
Crimes by Women
Crime Smasher
CRIMINALS – on the run
   (*formerly* King Cole)
Dick Tracy
Exposed
Famous Crimes
Gang Busters
GANGSTERS – can't win
Green Hornet (*new policy*)
Justice traps the GUILTY
GUNS – against Gangsters
International Crime Patrol
Jane Arden, Crime Reporter
Jeff Jordan, U.S. Agent
Joe Palooka (*new policy*)
The Killers
Law (against) Crime
LAWBREAKERS –
   always lose
Manhunt
March of Crime (25c)
Marvel Mystery
Mr. District Attorney
MURDER Incorporated
   ("For Adults Only")
On the Spot
This is the PAY-OFF
Crime must pay the
   PENALTY!

There is no escape for
   PUBLIC ENEMIES
Rip Kirby: Mystery of
   the Mangler
The Saint
Select Detective
Sky Sheriff
Special Agent
Top Secrets
True Crime
True (FBI Adventures)
Hard-hitting agents of
   the law strike at the
   UNDERWORLD
Vic Flint, Crime Buster
War Against Crime!
Whodunit
The Witness

All-American Western
All Western Winners
Annie Oakley
Bandit Trails
Black Cat (*new policy*)
Black Diamond
Blaze Carson
Blazing West
Brick Bradford
Broncho Bill
Charlie McCarthy,
   Cowboy Detective
Cowboy Western
Dale Evans, Queen of
   the Westerns
Dead-Eye Western
Desperado Desperado
Donald Duck: Sheriff
   of Bullet Valley
   (*new policy*)
Gabby Hayes Western
Gene Autry
Green Lantern (*new*:
   "Crime Goes West!")

Gunfighter
Gunsmoke
GUNS—of fact and fiction (*formerly* A-1)
Hopalong Cassidy
Jimmy Durante
Kid Colt, Outlaw
KING of the
   Royal Mounted
Little Beaver
The Lone Ranger
Monte Hale Western
Northwest Mounties
Outlaws
Prize Western (*third
   policy*)
Real Western Hero
"Red" Rabbit (*new
   policy*)
Roundup
Roy Rogers
Saddle Justice
Scribbly (*new policy*)
The Texan
Tex Farrell
Tex Granger (*formerly
   Calling All Boys*)
Tex Morgan
Tex Taylor
Tim Holt Western
Tim Tyler, Cowboy
Tom Mix Western
Two-Gun Kid
Western
Western Adventures
Western Fighters
Western Killers
Western Outlaws
Western Thrillers
Western True Crime
Wild West
Women Outlaws
Zane Grey

AVATARS OF THE BITCH

AVATARS OF THE BITCH

ONLY YESTERDAY men still imagined they were resting on the laurels of male domination. The lone, frightened voice of James Thurber seemed hardly more than amusing, eccentric. Man's cruelty to, and exploitation of woman is habitual. Men do not know that they are cruel. They see vaguely that all or most of the superior women around them are traumatized almost to the point of mania by their resentment and envy of men, yet men wonder how — now that women have the vote and the protection of the law — there can still be any war between the sexes. However, they still fight to the death every attempt on the part of women to attain economic or even merely human equality, shouting that they — the men — are being driven to the wall.

The moment has not yet come when women have passed the halfway mark and are driving any large number of men to the wall, but it can. And women know. And they dream. And they read. And, reading and dreaming, they fiercely delight in tales of triumphant bitchery, in which the immemorial tables are reversed, in which woman is master, and man the slave; in which man, the murderer, is murdered. As underdog, woman has crowned the bitch.

Until now the war between the sexes has been fought, on the literary plane at least, with men the attackers and women the defendants. Women have now begun their long-delayed counter-attack, and male writers are shouting to high heaven for justice. Actually, they have not yet sighted the battlefield, and are still slashing furiously at the air like blind Oedipus, calling down imprecations on their mothers' heads.

With the exception of Jane Collier's anonymous *The Art of Ingeniously Tormenting* in 1753, all defenses of themselves that women have written — as Rachel Speght (1617) and Mary Wollstonecraft (1792) — have been concerned for centuries either with rebutting the traditional allegations against them or with pleading their human rights. The idea of carrying the war into the camp of the enemy, man, is of so recent development that only the preliminary skirmishes have been fought, and these mostly in antique disguise.

LOVE & DEATH

The 'spirited' heroine — let us be frank, the *bitch*-heroine — appearing on the *champ de Mars* some twelve years ago, has carried popular literature before her; outselling, outswearing, and outswinging all competition. But she has not yet removed her mask. After a dozen years of spying out the land she still pretends to be merely an historical hussy, merely an exceptional vixen; or, if her methods are too bloodthirsty for the mild disguise of historical or individual peculiarity, she presents herself as a poor, helpless, pathological case. Let us not be fooled. She is no accident, neither of history, nor personality, nor pathology. She is a wishful dream — Venus Dominatrix — cunningly contrived out of the substance of women's longings. She is presented to the 'emancipated' but still enslaved wives-mothers-&-mistresses as a fantasy escape from their servitude to men, to fashion, traditional morality, and the paralyzing uselessness of being nothing but the show-horses of their owners' success.

The bitch-heroine speaks in a loud tone, moves with a firm stride; one hand always on the reins, the other ever-ready with the whip. She wants what she wants when she wants it, yes and by God she is going to get it (insert here a variety of 16th, 17th, or 18th century oaths), or she will whip, shoot, stab, scrounge, undermine, ruin, and drive to suicide, drink, or drugs any damn' man that stands in her way. Gadzooks and blast me! Call her Scarlett, call her Amber, call her Hotspur — she is still just the same damn' bitch.

Avatars of the bitch are many, the integers of her fantasy few. Once she is recognized for what she is, once the tattered historical panoply with which her creators furbish her up is discounted for what *it* is — gilt masquerade, easier to write than a modern milieu about which every reader might know something — the present profitable trickle of best-sellers through which she stamps can be pegged as formula-murder, long before this trickle will (as it must) become a flood.

So far as even the most lenient critical eye can see, the bitch-heroine is already as standard as the murder-mystery. Tear off her covers and slap them on some other volume of the kind, and no reader would know the difference. Except for the particular costume-&-century she wears, the bitch-heroine is mass produced. Her machine has only just gotten into operation: only one publisher (Macmillan), one reprint-house (Bantam), and two book-clubs (Fiction and Doubleday) as yet specialize in bitches; but soon we may expect to see her come popping off the presses daily — like the murder-mystery, her brother in blood.

THE BITCH-HEROINE

The bitch in literature is no new thing. She is Delilah, Salomé, Cressida, Cleopatra; Casanova's Charpillon, Sade's Juliette – the Medusa of the nineteenth century masochist-exotics – Baudelaire's half-Lesbian 'flower of evil,' Swinburne's flagellant Dolores, Mérimée's Carmen (and the imitation-Carmen of Pierre Louÿs' *Woman and Puppet*), the blood-lotus of Huysmans' *Là-bas* and Mirbeau's *Torture Garden*. The color of her hair is known. Her green eyes, cruel hands, the trembling of her lip – all old stuff. Cavaliere Mario Praz has anatomized her, complete with footnotes, in *The Romantic Agony* (chapter 4, "La Belle Dame Sans Merci"). Fuchs & Kind have gathered up her portraits in the three volumes of *Die Weiberherrschaft*. Our more sensitive writers have wrung her withers; snarled with Shakespeare, 'Oh Tyger's heart, wrapt in a woman's hide!' (3 *Henry VI*, I.iv.137.) Who else is Thackeray's Becky Sharp, Huxley's Lucy Tantamount, Hemingway's Lady Brett? Who else does Beerbohm lampoon – with her victims – in Zuleika Dobson, the *femme fatale* of a hundred shilling-shockers. The bitch has been here before. She was never gone. But, for our generation, first in *Gone With the Wind* in 1936 was she made a heroine. Margaret Mitchell did for bitchery what Edgar Allan Poe did for murder – she made it respectable. She, and Mrs. Wallis Warfield Simpson, for whose love (we are told) in the same year, a weakling king gave up his throne.

What was the message of the most phenomenally successful bestseller of the first half of the twentieth century – a book that sold fifty thousand copies on its first day of sale, millions since? Literary history will ask us. Why have we not yet set down the answer? The message of Margaret Mitchell's *Gone With the Wind* was hate. Nothing more. Hate, and war between the sexes from beginning to end, set – symbolically enough – against the background of another great civil war. Miss Mitchell's heroine ruins every man's life she touches, and that is what makes her a heroine. Utterly brainless, utterly shallow, vain, and useless – particularly in bed – Miss Mitchell's Venus Dominatrix wields the whip with a strong hand, figuratively over the back of every man who wants her sexually, and every woman who stands in her way; physically and in fact on a mere 'nigger' to the tune of *That's Why the Ku Klux Was Born*.

This flagellation scene, and the other in which the heroine shoots a revolver full in a 'rapist's' face, was of course retained in the million-dollar motion picture, that expurgated all but smirking morning-after implications of sex. Also served up in technicolor was the burning of

Atlanta, the first scene photographed – before even the leading lady was picked. Sex transvalued into pyromania. Ah brave new world, where Joe Breen calls the turn!

Miss Mitchell's recent crop of housewife-imitators – the Misses Winsor, Marshall, Rand, Bruff, Du Maurier, *et aliae* – are usually dismissed as merely illiterate, just as their best-sellers (and Miss Mitchell's) are casually written off as mere Victorian three-deckers, 'costume pornography,' of no critical importance save for the size of their heroine's breasts on the dust-jacket (*Life*, May 17th, 1948, pages 20-21). That they *are* bosomy masquerades, and frantically illiterate, I should be the last to deny; but in the face of their sales, the lack-or-knack of pattern style is irrelevant.

No one would suggest that such a book as Dale Carnegie's *How To Win Friends and Influence People* is literature on even the most abysmal level. Nor does its lack of literary quality matter in the least. What does matter is that two million people felt the need to buy such an agglomeration of measling, weasling deceitfulness, the gutter-guide to boot-licking and insincerity, the adaptation of the cheapest trickery of super-salesmanship to human relations. Books that sell two million copies would be important if they were written in pidgin-English and printed without punctuation. They are what the reading public is reading. And the discernment of just *what* it is reading – and why – matters.

The critical function has atrophied in America, or has been abdicated in favor of commercialism and commercialized snobbery, to the point where if fifteen hundred cowed intellectuals can be bamboozled into buying the latest tome on the latest fad: Kafka or Kierkegaard or Henry James, that is an event of cultural significance; while the daily – the hourly – murder and comic and bitch that one hundred and fifty million Americans must have, or perish, is of no importance.

Best-selling bitches are not altogether overlooked. They are too profitable for that; too profitable, too, for anything but the most superficial critical slobber. Piratical publishers, up to their ears in murder (psycho and plain), humorously castigate the 'hussy' heroine of competing publishers' lists – her huswifery consisting, to be sure, not in her flagellations and sadism, but in her 'lustfulness.' Literary puff- (and bull-) sheeters refer daringly to the 'five-letter female,' eructate their weekly yard of cant on her 'hysterical,' her 'bromidic,' sexuality. The ad is printed on the same page as the review.

THE BITCH-HEROINE

THERE IS in sex a normal component of sadism. It is not very large, and operates chiefly in courtship as a preliminary to coitus. It can never take the place of sex and still be called normal. The male pursues the female, and takes her cruelly. The female is cruelly coy, requiring of the male that he prove his superiority in combat with other males. In nature that is all there is to that. But by scorning and forbidding the ultimate conclusion intended for this in love and the creation of life, we have forced the cruel play of courtship to become the entire matter of the sexuality of our fiction, and — we now hear shouts & murmurs saying — of our lives.

Thus we have heroines who are coy to the point of mania, who require from men not the simple fact of male superiority to all other applicants, but agonies of submission, lumpish slavery, superhuman obedience to the female's every cruel or expensive whim. A man who will become a slave, merely for what sex an ordinary female can offer him, is a fool; and no one is more quickly aware of this than the female to whose tune he is idiotically dancing. She despises him, spurns him, turns to someone else, and begins all over.

In life this is as far as she can go. But in the fantasies of literature she can & does enact her dominance in more clearly physical ways, taking upon herself all the virility the man has forfeited, whipping him, torturing him, and finally doing him to death. The vampire — only halfway to bitchery — becomes passé. With all her aggressiveness, she is too female, too sexual. The bitch-heroine is neither. Enviously phallic, she can achieve her forlorn maleness only by castrating men.

But abnormality is always essentially tragic: all such stories develop a rough similarity. And their spiral ascends. Scarlett O'Hara ruined five men's lives. Duchess Hotspur, ten years later, runs through so many men she cannot remember their names, examines them in the nude before admitting them to her bed-chamber, can keep track of them only by cutting their initials on the leaves of her fan — a clear reminiscence of the cowboy killer and the notches on his gun. (This is the *Duchess Hotspur* — 'more exciting than Scarlett O'Hara... Yours as a gift' — offered free in a full-page, four-color ad in the comic-section of every Hearst newspaper on Sunday, September 15th, 1946; the same Duchess Hotspur — 'she arched to his embrace; from the zone of flame came an indescribable aura of seduction' — that Mr. Hearst arranged to run as a daily comic-strip, by way of climaxing his successful campaign for the suppression of Edmund Wilson's 'filthy' and 'indecent' *Memoirs of Hecate County*.)

LOVE & DEATH

These substitutions burgeon very quickly. They are unsatisfiable because they are abnormal and cannot be resolved. They have no logical end, therefore they do not end – except in death. Sadism installed as the substitute outlet for a forbidden sexuality, it reaches back and absorbs the deeper personality urges out of which sex should emerge as the fullest and final flowering. Sadism as the only shoot left standing, harks back for its nourishment to the personality taproots of sex, and appropriates to its own perverse augmentation all their flow: the sense of individuality, the desire for importance, attention, power; the pleasure in controlling objects, the impulse toward violent activity, the urge toward fulfillment to the farthest reach of the individual's biological possibilities. All these are restrained when sex is restrained, all these are congealed and perpetuated at the forceful, predatory courtship stage when coitus is forbidden to follow, all these are lacking in greater or less degree when sex is lacking, and they must be replaced in full.

Sadism – and in this its sinister attraction lies – allows all these impulses wildly more satisfaction than ever sex can. Sadistic flagellation is something more than a love-tap, and for good reason: When love is soon to follow, a tap will suffice. When love is forbidden, that tap must & will absorb into itself all the force intended for love, and grows and swells and balloons into a tumor of frustrate brutality, able to burst and fulfill itself only in the sadistic infliction of bondage, humiliation, terror, pain, and death; where the forbidden sexuality would have fulfilled itself in orgasm and the possible creation of life. We prefer sadism in our literature. We prefer death. The torturing of Clarissa Harlowe is "classic." The orgasm of Lady Chatterley is 'dirt.'

Satirically enough, the work of a man, not a woman, most strikingly displays our taboo on sex, our concomitant freedom for the merely sadistic bitch. Mr. Ben Ames Williams' *The Strange Woman* (1941) – 'her mouth is smoother than oil: But her end is bitter,' *Proverbs*, 5: 4 – is divided into seven sections, one for each man whose life she ruins. The seven are: her mother's lover (this while she is an infant in arms), her father, husband, step-son, second husband, a reformer, and her own son. Seven. By way of rounding out an even, sadist-incestuous *Beat Me, Mammy, Eight to the Bar*, Mr. Williams himself – her literary daddy – falls victim to his heroine's spirited vigor, avowing in his preface: 'Before the actual writing began, the central character assumed command.' This he repeats, after having had a year to think it over, in the preface to his *Time of Peace*:

THE BITCH-HEROINE

'The central character usurped that book (*The Strange Woman*) and to some extent defeated its original intent.'

The woman is not in the slightest degree strange. She is a sadist. She flagellates her children to the point of death, lamenting (page 487) that she has to stop there. She studies 'with a strange, still interest' (page 132) the 'red streak' left by the hangman's rope around the necks of executed pirates. She is 'transfigured ... her swimming eyes half-closed,' 'shivering in a sort of ecstasy' (page 65) by seeing a man squashed by an elephant. She is excited — ' "I like to hear about things like that," she said in her still, slow tones' — by hearing the description of a man killed by a falling tree, a description that makes a strong man 'sick' (page 66). A vampire as well as a sadist, she sucks blood from her baby's arm (page 288) for reasons she cannot explain — 'he was so sweet and soft and warm' she 'just couldn't help it.' On her death-bed, and from beyond the grave, she continues to enact her saleable, printable sadism in the form of a scandal-mongering will, to be printed 'in a prominent position' in the home-town newspaper.

Her *passions meurtrières*, and those of other, presumably non-pathological characters, appear once in every seven pages (72 scenes) of this 597-page book; sadism in combination with sex — to which it usually excites as in the 'ecstasy' above — once in every thirteen pages (39 scenes); sex *without* sadism in merely 27 scenes (once in every twenty pages), and of these more than half are incest! Ratio of sadism to sex: 3 to 1. About the only normal intercourse in the book is an accident — a boy imagines he is fornicating with the maid, but the heroine, his step-mother, has taken the maid's place in bed. This she does without passion, to force the boy to murder his father — the bitch-revision of *Hamlet* and *Oedipus*.

What happens to this sadist-incestuous garbage? Is it banned? It is not. Is it banned at least in Boston? No, it is *published* in Boston, and by a publisher so strait-laced and honorable as to pay royalties to Hitler on *Mein Kampf*. It becomes a best-seller and stays a best-seller for five years. Two million copies are sold.

Then must come the movie. Immortalized on film by Miss Hedy LaMarr and United Artists at an advertised cost of two million dollars, the unreeling of this 'strange' life story is arranged for New York's show-case theater, the Astor, on Christmas Day. (*Variety*, November 6th, 1946, page 3, column 5, headline: 'Selznick Lost It At the Astor.') No objection is expected from the New York motion picture censorship that found *The Birth of a Baby* obscene.

LOVE & DEATH

Is that all? Not quite. Mr. Williams then does it all over again in *Leave Her to Heaven* (sic), concerning a young lady who becomes so uncontrollably erotic at her father's funeral (n.b.) that she picks up a stranger, breaks off her engagement to her fiancé (one down, three to go), marries the stranger and drowns his brother, a cripple (two down), throws herself down the stairs to kill her boy-baby when she is pregnant (three down), and finally commits suicide – arranging for it to seem like murder by her sister, to whom her husband, a writer, has gone and dedicated his novel (incest). The sister is acquitted (a woman, you know), and the husband goes to jail for concealing evidence of his wife's crime (four down). There has also been a movie made from this. It is 'psychological.' 'Psychological' movies – always about murder – are very popular just now.

Following deep in Mr. Williams' footsteps are one Henning, author of *The Heller* (1947) – i.e. bitch – with cover-design by the author showing a giant female in her slip tossing around pigmy males, and a Mr. Frank Yerby, one eye reputedly fixed on the goal of being the first Negro writer to make a million dollars. His method: white bitches – three in a row – his latest, published under the euphemism of *The Vixens,* having been announced originally as *Ignoble Victory*. (And compare Daddy Williams' *Hostile Valley,* pocket-reprinted as *Valley Vixen.*)

It is not always possible to distinguish between the bitch-creations of masochists like Swinburne and Louÿs, and the commercial products of the best-seller mill. Nor, so far as the readers are concerned, is it necessary. The impact on the experiencing mind is the same. It will be seen, however, that Ben Ames Williams takes up where the Marquis de Sade left off, adding to the pleasures of cruelty the delights of incest, with which Rétif de La Bretonne hopefully imagined he could counteract Sade's influence. Mr. Williams also extends the province of the sadist's activity both beyond death and before life, his heroines beginning their bitchery in cradle or womb, and continuing it necrosadistically from the coffin.

•

PARADOX grips us. If murder is right and sex is wrong, we shall be running out of victims very shortly. Soon there will be no one left to murder but ourselves. This may be the only solution.

THE BITCH-HEROINE

In the past only poets and physicians have tried to halt our march toward death. 'Not Death,' sang Elizabeth Barrett Browning, 'but Love.' Help is now arriving, a century late, from a somewhat unexpected quarter. The murder-mystery has discovered sex. And frenziedly, perhaps only to point up the now rather oft-repeated tale of slaughter, perhaps out of justifiable anxiety to tap the 'sex-mad' market, intransigeant mystery-writers attempt to mix eroticism with their murder; thus, as it were, replacing their victims, setting them up again in the next alley — a conservation program for death.

They strain for 'realism,' by which, says realist James T. Farrell, they mean an 'utterly pointless and unilluminating . . . suggestion of extra-marital sexual relationships . . . with a few touches of vernacular dialogue.' (*The League of Frightened Philistines*, 1945, page 182 n.) But what happens? As with two nearly similar colors placed side by side, the weaker disappears. Sex intruded into the murder-mystery turns ice-cold. It has no body, sets no tone, vanishes immediately the moment the author stops lugging it onstage; and it is not missed. It is sex only at the shallowest level of rough vocabulary and pallid incident.

The case of Dashiell Hammett, in whose work the current trend toward sex combined with bloodlust took form — under the euphemism 'hard-boiled' — is illuminating. Hammett's real contribution to the murder-mystery was that he dropped the oldstyle moron-narrator of Poe and Doyle, and made easier the reader's self-identification with the detective by telling the story in the first person as the manhunter himself. But it is for his attempted combination of coitus and killing — the essence of the Marquis de Sade's lethography — that he is principally imitated.

Shyly pioneering, the sex in *The Thin Man* (1934) — the highwater mark of Hammett's 'eroticism' — is wholly conversational. No one goes to bed with anyone, but everyone talks endlessly about who has been 'playing around' and 'living with' whom, all of this having happened before the book opens. Even so, Hollywood timidly transposed what there was of this paper-thin sexuality into the piddling-pup & toilet-seat type of juvenile scatology which is for some reason less censorable than love, and which, overemphasized to make up for the 'sex' removed, made the movie a smash success. The actual scatology of murder — the *grumus merdae* of a defiant turd in the dresser drawer — is, of course, too real for the necrophil 'realism' of the murder-mystery. (Dr. Theodor Reik: *The Unkown Murderer*, 1945, chapter 8, "The 'Visiting-Card'.")

E

LOVE & DEATH

Hammett's worst written and most popular book, *The Thin Man* was ballyhooed into best-sellerdom with specific reference in its advertising to the furore-arousing page – 192 – on which a wife scandalously asks her detective-husband if he didn't 'have an erection' in wrestling with the epileptic villainess. And though 'no legal steps . . . were ever taken or threatened against this book at any time whatever' (letter from Mr. Alfred A. Knopf, December 31st, 1946), the Pocket Book reprint, ten years later, retains all the foreground of murder – and the very extensive background of drunkenness, flagellation, cannibalism (chapter 13), and unachieved incest – but changes this legal and unexceptionable passage to read: 'get excited.' No word concerning this expurgation appears anywhere on any one of the one million copies of the Pocket Book 25c. reprint, which is advertised instead as 'Complete & Unabridged.' Eight stiffened corpses – good. One penis (ditto) – bad.

James M. Cain's numerous homicidal females and meacock males freely slap, stab, shoot, and sic lions on one another, but their much-deplored motivating sexuality (no one deplores their murderousness and greed) is strictly of a background nature, seldom more than modestly detailed, and that usually in reference to the breasts. And though Mr. Cain brags, in the introduction to his recent incest-thriller, *The Butterfly,* that where Hemingway sometimes 'uses four-letter words (that is, those dealing with bodily functions); I have never written one' – what, never?! – Hollywood finds even this prophylactic sex too much for its audience, cutting all but the uncensorable sex-hatred and violence from dialogue and plot in transferring Cain's murders to the screen, and retaining the breast fetishism only insofar as this can be wordlessly communicated by sixty-foot billboards displaying Miss Lana Turner's bosom.

Harry Kurnitz' *Fast Company* (published under the pseudonym 'Marco Page' – there is no prejudice in this country) is as methodically larded with off-color remarks and suggestions as a musical-comedy; but, though sexual intercourse take place twice – again between husband & wife – none of this is able in the least to raise the tone of the book from murder to anything else. The detective-husband carefully recollects the secrets of his bed-chamber to the reader's attention by remarking to his wife: 'I did not kill Abe Selig. I did my good deed in the morning before I came to work. Remember?' (which should make the substitution relationship between love and death clear to even the dimmest mentality), and prefigures their second in-

THE BITCH-HEROINE

timacy with 'This is the one that drove the Sultan mad.' As sex, however, the book never gets off the ground. Nor is there any record that the movie version was at all unpopular in those certain states where Mr. Melvyn Douglas was not allowed to mumble: 'Hey what's the meaning of this in broad daylight, and you the woman who wouldn't let me buy a couch for the office.' Except for Jack the Ripper (Dr. Alexander Pedachenko) and his kind, sex and murder do not sympathetically combine.

Similarly confected on the Hollywood synthetic-sex pattern is Richard Sale's *Lazarus #7,* a Bible-spouting anti-Semitic tract, with a few utterly lifeless and thoroughly expurgated sexual suggestions thrown in ('noisier than skeletons *cop'latin'* on a tin roof' – chapter 22). Alternating between virginal talky-talk concerning unachieved seductions, and the Babylon-denouncing prurience of the 23rd chapter of Ezekiel, the purpose of most of the 'sex' here is to depict a vulgar Jewish movie-producer (named Roach) as a leering, breast-pawing swine. By way of anticlimax to the usual murderer-suicide, this Jew is lynched – in the form of a good Nordic smash in the jaw – as the ultimate thrill for both reader and, blatantly, the author.

The Smell of Money by 'Matthew Head' (John Canaday) is pronounced by all experts the sexiest item as yet peddled on the murder-market. Its sex consists solely of several undescribed acts of intercourse between narrator and murderess, and a single use of the phrase 'sleep with' by an elderly woman. The murderess is the wife of a sadistic homosexual, clearly described (he keeps her for trading purposes only, with a hint at seminal exsufflation in the bushes), who, for her crimes, cuts off her hands at the wrists and leaves her to bleed to death on a pink rug. He is in love with the narrator himself. The entire sixteenth chapter is then spent apologizing for the 'amorality' of the adultery preceding. Homosexual sadism – not to mention murder, and the wholesale greed upon which, as indicated in the title, the book is based – does not require apology.

In England 'James Hadley Chase' (René Raymond) boldly plagiarizes both violence and sex from Hemingway's *To Have and Have Not* for his background in *Twelve Chinks and a Woman,* and from Faulkner's *Sanctuary* in *No Orchids for Miss Blandish,* his plot in each case turning upon a nymphomaniac-*cum*-masochist, his detective hero 99 44/100% impervious to her somewhat equivocal charms. *No Orchids* was attacked in England for its sex (literary sadism is not illegal), and *Twelve Chinks and a Woman* was cut to the bone of all

LOVE & DEATH

sex when reprinted in America for 15c. – 'edited to convenient reading length,' it says here – on the theory that no one would miss it; but none of its brutality, including the slapping of a woman's bare breasts on page 22 (reprint edition), seemed unreprintable. If they had been kissed instead, this would no doubt have been obscene.

A great deal of noisy indignation was stirred up among British murder-fanciers by 'Chase's' ungentlemanly intrusion of sex into the chaste annals of death and brutality. Eric Partridge refuses even to publicize this author by his pseudonym, referring to him instead under the elegant periphrasis: 'that unnamed sensationalist ... who refused Miss Blandish the dubious consolation of even a few bespattered orchids.' (*Journey to the End of the Morning*, 1946, page 26.) While in *Dickens, Dali & others* (1946, page 221), 'George Orwell' – these *skiomachiai!* pseudonym against pseudonym – dealt the final, crushing blow of finding the atmosphere of *No Orchids* to compare infelicitously with the exemplary snobbishness of E. W. Hornung's cricket-playing *Raffles*: 'In Mr. Chase's book there are no gentlemen, and no taboos. Emancipation is complete, Freud and Machiavelli have reached the outer suburbs.'

Vivian Connell's *The Chinese Room,* an English importation, attempts to soften the fact of its being a sex novel by threading in a murder-plot as well, but our unofficial censor, Mr. Sumner, was not fooled. At his suggestion the book was withdrawn without trial, the half-price and pocket reprints omitting a three-line reference to fellation (though retaining – ignorance, pure ignorance – a more recherché hint at cunnilinctus with chocolates). The murder-plot remains.

Taking their cue from a genially horrified plug in *Time* magazine, Farrar & Rinehart imported and published, complete – six years after its publication in England – Gerald Butler's kills-&-thrills murder-shocker, *Kiss the Blood Off My Hands,* simultaneously achieving the all-time high of art expurgation in Abner Dean's *It's a Long Way to Heaven* (imitated from William Steig), in which are included drawings of three hundred and twenty-three – 323 – naked men, not one of them anatomically male. Sex being so taboo and murder so respectable, one wonders if the two might not be combined somehow to respectabilize the first, perhaps in some such title as *Kiss the Blood Off My* —— but no, it would be impossible.

Disguising his repugnance with difficulty, another rough-tough murder retailer, Raymond Chandler, brings sex into his principal volume backwards, through persistent negation; basing *The Big Sleep*

THE BITCH-HEROINE

(1939) – title, style, and detective clearly patterned on Hammett's – on a pornographic lending-library business operated by a homosexual who is murdered for taking nude photographs of a drugged débutante. But this absurd plot-mélange is the total of achieved sexuality anywhere in the book. Even the swearing is expurgated with pudibund dashes – Knopf edition, page 122. The evil female protagonists are all lecherous as so many minks, leaping naked in & out of the detective's bed and arms, but this shamus-Galahad is adamantly pure. He never lays so much as the proverbial finger on Chandler's loose-kneed villainesses, and he detests the pornography he must handle, must even – perish the thought! – disguise himself as a homosexual and pretend to sell. (Chapter 10. Mr. Chandler seems to be sold on the proposition that homosexuals have the pornography business tied up.) An imitator, 'William Francis' Urell, similarly sets his *Rough On Rats* against a backdrop of the pornographic motion picture industry – a prop repeated in "Cloak Across the Blood" in *Esquire,* Thanksgiving 1948 – but *his* detective-Parsifal eventually burns up all the erotic films involved, without even peeping at them, after sufficiently roughing up the rats that made them.

One explanation for all this heroic purity is offered by Chandler in "The Simple Art of Murder" (De Quincey called it a *fine* art) in the *Atlantic Monthly,* December 1944, in a four-hundred-word perorational plug for his own detective-hero, in which we learn that he is,

> to use a rather weathered phrase, a man of honor, by instinct, by inevitability, without thought of it, and certainly without saying it.... I do not care much about his private life; he is neither a eunuch nor a satyr; I think he might seduce a duchess and I am quite sure he would not spoil a virgin.

To date, neither seduced duchesses nor unspoiled virgins have appeared in Chandler's writing. No sexual intercourse takes place. His women are all strictly flaming bitches, killers, or corpses. Thus *The Lady in the Lake:*

> The thing rolled over once more and an arm flapped up barely above the skin of the water and the arm ended in a bloated hand that was the hand of a freak. Then the face came. A swollen pulpy gray white mass without features, without eyes, without mouth. A blotch of gray dough, a nightmare with human hair on it.

With this excursion into anti-female necrophilia (now a movie, of course), compare the following from *Farewell, My Lovely,* chapter 35:

> His voice was soft, dreamy, so delicate for a big man that it was startling. It made me think of another soft-voiced big man I had strangely liked . . . I looked at him again. He had the eyes you never see, that you only read about. Violet eyes. Almost purple. Eyes like a girl, a lovely girl. His skin was as soft as silk . . . it would never tan. It was too delicate. He was bigger than Hemingway and younger. . .

And yet, no matter how 'strangely' Chandler's detective, Marlowe, moons over these big men, they are always beating him up; a new departure, certainly, in fictional detectives, and a little hard on the reader or movie-goer explicitly invited – no, *forced* (by protagonist-camera film techniques: 'YOU and Robert Montgomery in *The Lady in the Lake*') – to identify himself with the detective. The true explanation of Marlowe's temperamental disinterest in women is not 'honor,' but his interest in men. Like another more famous Marlowe, who died avowing 'That all thei that love not Tobacco & Boies were fooles,' Chandler's Marlowe is clearly homosexual – a butterfly, as the Chinese say, dreaming that he is a man.

Whatever its reason, through this technique of persistent sexual negation, every detail of ravishing female nudity, lascivious temperament, &c. can be gone into at any desired length – as John Del Torto points out – so long as the whole is purified and antisepticized by the detective-hero's frigid rejection. But this very rejection cools the ardor so carefully ignited (it is hoped) when overlaying a sexual situation upon the necessary murder or murders. The bitch-heroine rises to solve the difficulty. *Her* transvalued sexuality flourishes best, like Lady Macbeth's – fit reading for school-children once Shakespeare's single sexual lapse from murder (the Porter scene, II. iii. 23-34) is expurgated – in the icy atmosphere of blood and killing. Her masterful excitements are not fazed by murder, but rather heightened all the more.

●

As do the adult comic-strips, that respectabilize with an overlay of violence (Pow! Wham! Socko!!) whatever hints of sexual love they must intrude with the inevitable hen-pecked, dog-housed, bitch-bitten

THE BITCH-HEROINE

husband – Jiggs, the old clown, or uxorious young Dagwood well on his way toward becoming a Jiggs – just so the murder-mystery, having discovered sex, now discovers a less pallid sexual pattern in the maniacal male-protest and overt sadism of the bitch-heroine. (Erle Stanley Gardner's 'A. A. Fair' brace of detectives, for example – meek little Donald Lamb and his employer, Bertha 'Behemoth' Cool – are simply Maggie & Jiggs adapted to the needs of the murder-loving public. A three-hundred-pound bitch, however, is almost too much of a good thing.)

The usual form in which she is presented – by men – still drawing on Hammett's inspiration, is as the detective's wife, necessarily outshining him in bloodthirstiness, and passing quickly from mere wife through co-detective (a favorite device with husband-wife murder-writing teams, of which there are several) to her final elevation as chief operative, making a monkey out of her blundering spouse. The last effort by 'S. S. Van Dine' – through whom the murder-mystery came of age in America – was one of these: *The Gracie Allen Murder Case*, tailor-made to the pattern imbecility of a 'dumb'-bitch comedy team. Reverting almost to femaleness, comes now the pregnant lady dick in Manning Long's *Savage Breast* (1948), an incredible mish-mash of murder and obstetrics with the seven-months' pregnant wife chasing around town after the murderer.

More typical is Richard Pitts Powell's Arab, a flighty blonde gun-fancier who can't cook anything but gunpowder; and her husband, Andy, a self-confessed gibbering coward who is slugged, mugged, beaten, browbeaten, womanhandled, shot, kicked, and half-killed yearly by author Powell and his high-spirited Arab in one or another volume of 'mystery.' This annual husband-murdering is obviously the equivalent of Scarlett O'Hara's succession of male victims, but within the framework of respectable monogamy and the detective-series game. According to his blurbs, Mr. Powell is very popular with readers of *The Ladies' Home Journal*.

In his *Lay That Pistol Down* (Pistol-Packin' Mama) there is not even a motivating murder, so far does the gun-girl's sadism transcend mere death. The unpatriotic villain is horribly dispatched in the end – through his own machinations, of course – without having consummated any killing to speak of but his own. His real villainy consists in being a 'wolf.' He *leers* at women, and combs his hair frequently. The title-page of the Bantam Book reprint of this volume (1946) is decorated prominently with a picture of a woman shooting off an

LOVE & DEATH

enormous duelling pistol from between her legs. ('She doesn't like pistols that just peck holes. She likes ones that excavate.' – chapter 3.) Since nothing even remotely of this sort occurs in the text, there is possibly some recondite symbolism involved.

Until Mr. Powell and the other hard-working Judases of the male sex came along, female man-eaters had been the special province of lady murder-writers, and a profitable one too. The best-selling author since Shakespeare is Mary Roberts Rinehart – her formula: multiple murders, told by a woman. Carrying the formula into her own life, Mrs. Rinehart's ghastly autobiography, *My Story*, is bloodier than any of her fiction; most of her family, pets, and friends having died tragically and suddenly. (Lest there be any misunderstanding, Mrs. Rinehart's alibi is in every case perfect, her intentions pluperfect. In fact, Had She But Known, they might all have been saved.)

Stemming clearly from Mrs. Rinehart's hooch-swigging 'Tish' – a great favorite during Prohibition – are the even boozier murder-idylls of Miss 'Craig Rice,' her various male pseudonyms fortified by her photograph in her husband's coat & tie, crêpe beard, pipe, and slouch hat (in *Time*, January 28th, 1946, page 84), her specialty the perverting of popular proverbs to the light-minded mood of drunken murder, as in *Having Wonderful Crime*, concerning the decapitation of a rich Lesbian by her husband-*de-covenance* on her wedding night.

A dozen cuts above Rinehart and Rice is Dorothy Sayers, the most capable writer (of any sex) in a profession where hackwork illiteracy is almost an unbroken rule. The reason is probably that Miss Sayers is not really a murder-writer at all, but a bitter feminist, killing off men on paper – preferably husbands & lovers – and in the weakly feminine way of poison. In the culmination of her art, *Gaudy Night* (which, lacking a murder, concerns itself with 'the crime of disseminating obscene libels [in] a community of celibate women'), the whole plot turns on the fact that an educated woman is better able to ruin a man's life than is the vulgar and untutored scrublady he marries.

Miss Sayers is the wife of a war-correspondent and hero, and may be assumed to have unconsciously embraced the anti-feminist standard she thinks she is fighting: that men are everything, and women nothing. Accordingly, all her man-quelling is achieved in the character of an hermaphrodite called Harriet Vane – Lord Peter Wimsey, which makes gelid love to itself occasionally by way of convincing both author and cash-customers that it is really two people hotly in love with each other. Actually, Lord Peter – by & large the most disgust-

THE BITCH-HEROINE

ing snob in English literature – is Harriet Vane in pants, the man Harriet Vane (same number of syllables as Dorothy Sayers) desperately wishes she were. When she is in jail, as in *Strong Poison*, he even does her detecting for her, as a sort of male-protest Doppelgänger, 'changing, changing' – like the poisoned Athulf in Beddoes' *Fool's Tragedy* – 'fearfully changing.' With Harriet-Peter's marriage to itself in *Busman's Honeymoon* – consummated by tracking down a juicy murder or so, instead of in the usual way – Miss Sayers' hermaphroditic bitch identified itself completely with the male and disappeared from the market, leaving its author to seek forgiveness for her paper-poisonings in religion and good works.

But men make the best prostitutes in the end. Just as Ben Ames Williams was able to out-bitch all the lady authors in their own 'historical' field, another gentleman has topped the ladies in limning the 'mystery'-bitch as well. In Cornell Woolrich's *The Bride Wore Black* (1940), the murder-mystery rises to a second *Gone With the Whip* in the unremitting technique of sex-hatred. A virgin-bride is brought in as avenger, in place of the usual detective, and the reader is invited to project sympathetically into her man-hunting. She tracks down and kills four completely innocent men, and tries to dispose of a fifth apparently only so that she may be caught and the usual sop (one more death: her own) be thrown to 'justice.'

Studiously gruesome, her killings are described in attractive detail as she achieves them: #1 she pushes to his death from a 17th-floor terrace, #2 she poisons, #3 she smothers alive in an oak closet with walls two inches thick, #4 she shoots through the heart with a bow & arrow, and prepares death for #5 in a sawed-off shotgun aimed at the back of his neck. All her victims are innocent of any mortal offense, but – and this is the key – their murdering is in every case effected strictly and absolutely, and on a *sine qua non* basis, through the sex-appeal of the murderess-avenger. For the bow-&-arrow killing she actually strips naked (the victim is an artist), trembling in shame at her virgin nudity; unabashed, however, at dealing death.

To make her list of sex-achieved murders complete, the very husband whose death this latter-day Dumas heroine is avenging, was killed in the first place by her own demand that he change his (criminal) way of life in order to be worthy of her, and that he marry her showily in church. Conversely, the only unsympathetic character in the book – even the policeman who puts her away in the end, closes the handcuff around her wrist 'almost gently' – is the one man who

LOVE & DEATH

escapes her vengeance, and he is painted in his blackest dye by making him out a lecher and a 'wolf,' that is to say, by having him annoy the killer-bitch with his sexual urgencies without offering her any other inducement to kill him.

In spite of all this insistence upon the positively aphrodisiacal aura surrounding the female sadist — whether in the murder-mystery or in her chosen 'historical' vehicle — there is no disguising the fact that she is pretty cold potatoes. The Venus of the Loaded Revolver is hardly Venus.

Understand that the bitch-heroine has no sex. She *thinks* she has a great deal of sex, in which error her creators and consumers foolishly accompany her. She is punctiliously put forward as a saucy baggage, a pert minx, a froward wench, headstrong, conceited, spoiled, arrogant, and similar terms of sexual approbation, her malicious wilfulness presumably an exciting challenge to conquest for the more dunderheaded sort of male.

Inevitably she is described as ravishing and beautiful. Her breasts and genitals are commented upon in high calorific terms. But in actual fact she is dead from the neck down. She is a sadist — a flagellator — and all her sexual impulse has long since been soured into vanity and hate. Cruelty is her life; fiercely dominant, her notion of love can be enacted only with whips and revolvers. Her sexual part — Duchess Hotspur alternates between calling it her 'red mouse' and 'the warm well of her' — has no sensations of its own, no meaning to its possessor. It is simply a bait to catch male victims — a decoy, a fool-trap, a red herring, a painted rubber duck.

The various pothers about the immorality of *Gone With the Wind, Forever Amber, Duchess Hotspur,* &c., entirely overlook the fact that these books and their heroines have no more sexual thrill in them than so many iced fish. Nor is it their intention to create sexual delight in the reader, at least not in any recognizable, forthright pornographic way. The commodity they are selling is hatred.

Their heroines go through the motions of sexuality, usually wholesale, merely by way of retaliation for what their authoresses believe to be the habits of men. Their true thrill, however, is in destroying the lives and life-illusions of as many men as possible. The acme of the bitch-heroine's invariable achievement is not sexual intercourse — not even orgasm, in a culture where psychiatric quacks are able to peddle super-orgasms — but the dragging down of some man's deepest dream to shit on it.

THE BITCH-HEROINE

BUT WHY? Women have made and continue to make the tactical error of *accepting the enemy's values.* Consciously or unconsciously they allow themselves to be convinced that being a woman is bad, that being a man is *per se* good, and that only those things are worth doing, that, by the rather obvious subterfuge of keeping women out, men have been able to do better. The reaction is either to try to be a man – pants, penis, and all the rest of it – and do what men do; or, failing that, to claw down the nearest male by whatever means one can, and so be faced with no invidious comparison. In essence, this is the bitch. Seen in this light she is a bitch only so far as her victim is concerned. For herself, she is tortured and torn.

Loaded down with her trumpery baubles, her mouth rouged and glycerined to look like her twat, one hand immobilized with a purse reduplicating the symbol, her hair upswept (or down) and her skirt hobbled at the dictates of one Parisian fairy, her breasts bare or roped flat at the behest of another, teetering on high heels in four-strap fetichist footwear for the amusement of a third (Helen Brown Norden "Fashion Is a Fairy," in *The Hussy's Handbook,* 1942, pages 165-174), prodded at by lackwit mothers to sell her hymen quickly to the highest bidder, and battered at by whoring ad-men – one lesson ahead of her in the psychology book – with a continuous, needling barrage to the effect that she is ugly, old, wrinkled, sag-breasted, broad-buttocked, and smelly in the crotch; it is not easy for any woman to feel superior. Only a gentleman-sociologist can be so taken in by this formalized inculcation of an inferiority complex for women as to imagine that the fact of all eyes being naggingly and incessantly upon her makes her the honorific 'cynosure' of our society (Prof. Weston La Barre, in *Journal of Personality,* 1946, vol. 14: pages 169-183).

Women are told that they are free. And yet they are not free. What freedom they have achieved in these last hundred years has been grudging, embittered, contradicted at every turn by man's continuing arrogation of superiority to himself. Their legal disabilities have been removed (in some countries: in others, wives are still brought home in chains), but nowhere and in no sense have men accepted them as equals. What man would change places with what woman?

Ten thousand years' training in inferiority is not so easy to efface. Too fearful for open revolt, woman waits out her night in envious and bloody imaginings. Man is the enemy, his penis the point in excellence of his enmity. Feared and hated, it becomes the ultimate desirable: with that lever she could move the world. Lacking it, her reaction is to call it names, whittle it down to peewee size, castrate it altogether in fantasy – it and the dreams and achievements that are its symbolic equivalent.

No more appalling demonstration of this reaction to the continuous onslaught against a woman's self-respect can be found than in the latest and bitterest of the formal attacks on men that women are now writing, Ruth Herschberger's *Adam's Rib* (1948). Miss Herschberger is justifiably angry at the prejudice that leads male writers to refer to the clitoris as a vestigial penis, instead of – as they might – to the penis as a hypertrophied clitoris, and spends a charming satirical chapter ("Society Writes Biology") on reversals of this sort, another – p. 20, technique included – on "Can Women Rape Men?" At the same time, she so far accepts the enemy standard of mere size as to maintain that since, under the microscope, the clitoris has nerve-endings four times thicker than those of the penis (total thickness: one and one-half millimetres), the clitoris is bigger & better; and she marvels at the 'incredible feat that society should actually have convinced the possessors of this organ that it was sexually inferior to the penis.' There is even a semantic plot involved, Miss Herschberger feels, in that – by strict etymological principles – 'clitoris' should really be pronounced with a long vowel, *clite-oris,* and 'penis' with a short one: *pennis.* 'One likes to envisage the difficulty Freud might have run into,' she concludes (chapter 4), 'if he had to prove the universal existence of something called *pennis envy*.'

Not every woman is so grotesquely candid. Tearfully weak, most women find it easier to effect the necessary castration symbolically, unconsciously; running off, not with the envied penis, but – by a foolish metonymy – with the pants. In photograph after photograph in her otherwise sober vindication of women, *Three Guineas* (1938), Virginia Woolf holds up to well-earned ridicule 'A General,' 'A Judge,' 'An Archbishop,' and so forth – but all of them are in skirts. When Mrs. Woolf herself is photographed, in her *Orlando* (1928), she vacillates between women's clothes and men's. Similarly Elizabeth Hawes, who tabulates with bitter fairness in *Anything But Love* (1948) the pulverization of American women by all the suggestion-pressure of society, but who, in her position as clothing-designer, is not above the unconscious connivery of trying to put men into skirts. (*Men Can Take It,* 1939, page 255.) Meanwhile, since 1933, under the same transparent rationalizations of 'comfort' and aestheticism – and in defiance of Bible (*Deuteronomy,* 22:5), law, and custom –

THE BITCH-HEROINE

pants for women sweep the western world. Whatever Miss Hawes' motives may have been, when American schoolgirls blossom out, million-strong, in their brothers' shirts, over skin-tight dungarees with a copper-riveted clitoris on the fly, it is not in response to any epidemic urge for comfort. It is because they want the status that goes with pants.

Men are very jealous of their genital haberdashery — their pants and hats and ties and smoking utensils — and resist with humorless intensity any encroachment by women upon the unearned prerogatives that these symbols represent. (All the hateful jokes about women's slacks and hats, women drivers, women who smoke, women in bars, *etc. ad naus.*) It would seem men are somehow aware that these symbols are all they have left. Behind the stalking-horse of pants — behind all the other ancient dodges: that Eve tempted Adam in paradise with a banana, that women have no 'genius,' no brains, no souls, that women do not produce art (any more than do the generality of men) — the technological basis of man's domination of woman has moved out from under him.

There is in nature — let us go cautiously here — there *seems* to be in nature more difference between the sexes than their matching anatomical disparity, more difference than that one does nature's work for ten seconds, the other for ten lunar months. (And by whose standard is the ten seconds' spasm active and prideful — Have a cigar! — the ten months' ripening passive, bovine, and more than vaguely a reproach?) It is not here, in the principal business of the human race, but rather in the peripheral display leading up to it that man's superiority to woman is presumed to reside. But the domination of women by men has nothing to do with this, nothing to do with right or wrong or merit. It is not based on any 'innate' artistic superiority of sixty million salesclerks and mechanics over sixty million housewives and typists. It does not rise from any 'natural' reason why everything human in the human animal should be the province of man, everything else the duty of woman. It was achieved by force — with metal tools and war and the impregnability of women — and has been maintained by the planned psychological destruction of women's characters for ten thousand years. And it is nearly over.

In the brittle mechanisms of typewriter and birth-control, the technology that now discards man, has freed woman — where all the pamphleteers and feminists had failed. In the face of the machine man finds himself almost useless, ready to be scrapped, passed by in strength and brains. Woman remains: incorruptible, irreplaceable. Safely in her own hands, the fertility that once made her weak and 'unclean' (but twice as unclean for a girl-child as for a boy; *Leviticus*, 12:2-5) now sets her beyond the competition of any machine; while, for man's part, biologists envisage "Human Parthenogenesis and the Elimination of the Male." (Remy de Gourmont: *The Natural Philosophy of Love*, 1917, chapter 7.) Against this prospect, the 'superior' man that women are so busy competing with, is seen to be a phantom.

With the return of the mother as the dominant parent, certain other reversals must follow: Oedipus disappears, the father he was competing with now become a punching-bag and clown. Electra comes sullenly onstage, the same father — and, with him, all men — now utterly forbidden by her mother's newfound strength. Like the homosexual, who cannot have a love-relationship with men, and must satisfy himself with hate — with beatings-up in public toilets by sailors and rough trade — Electra finds open to her only the furious passions of violence and strife. The legs entwine, breasts heave together, mouths strike, hair tangles — but this is hate, not love, and the jealous parent is allayed.

The parallel between homosexuality in men and frigidity in women is worth exploring. In both of them the dynamic is fear. Briefly stated, the homosexual male is one in whom

> the fear of the father is the most powerful psychic motive ... In his imagination all women belong to the father, and he seeks refuge in men out of submission, so as to 'retire from' the conflict in favor of the father. (Sigmund Freud: "Psychogenesis of a Case of Homosexuality ..." 1920, *Collected Papers*, vol. 2: page 216, note 2.)

The homosexual naturally does not refer to himself as weak, and to his father as fearsome. No, he 'respects' his father, 'idolizes' male strength, is 'thrilled' by guns and knives, men in uniform, boxers, bull-fighters, and all the other impedimenta and personalia of virility; searches out specimens with the largest possible genitals upon which to lavish his love. Women are 'bad.' His mother is bad. She does not love or 'understand' his father. Instead of fantasying himself replacing his father in his mother's arms, the homosexual fantasies himself as a woman replacing his mother in his father's arms — taking upon him-

THE BITCH-HEROINE

self female clothing if he dares. Only in this way can his father's jealous anger be turned safely into love. For the more virile crypto-homosexual, the Oedipal conflict can be more direct. He can himself become soldier, boxer, bull-fighter or what not, and kill his father time after time, overcompensating his evasion of the real conflict in his endless repetition of the symbolic death. But the fearful denigration and rejection of the mother – and, with her, all women – is never given up.

In a patriarchal society, a woman in the situation that makes a man homosexual does not have the refuge of Lesbianism open to her. Where woman is without status, Lesbianism is obviously factitious and not a little absurd. The unwilling Electras can 'respect' their mothers, and call their fathers 'weak,' but they cannot love women. Castaways of the interregnum, their motion is wholly negative – away from femininity and toward frigidity – the transvestism that is the smallest part of the homosexual's activity necessarily the largest part of theirs.

> Out of spite and resentment they refuse to enjoy coitus. They look upon a mother as a dangerous person, injurious to everyone. Another important factor in the frigid reaction is the . . . idea that the mother's sexual life with the father cannot be pleasurable. This belief is caused by the feeling that their own hostility may have interfered with her sexual pleasure. In fantasy they actually did try to hinder her enjoyment. Their flight from femininity is a reaction to this aggression and consequent fear of the mother. (Sándor Lorand: "Contribution to the Problem of Vaginal Orgasm," in *International Journal of Psychoanalysis*, 1939, vol. 20: page 438.)

Recognized as Electra, the bitch-heroine becomes finally understandable in her cold sex and hot brutality. She is not frigid because she hates men, nor cruel in revenge. But only in frigidity is she safe from her mother's jealousy; and, sex being forbidden, there is only sadism left. Meanwhile, the passing of the Oedipus complex, with the end of the father's dominance, makes typical the unvirile, masochistic male who is the bitch's perfect match. In view of the self-perpetuating equilibrium thus achieved, dreams of the equality of the sexes seem far-off and utopian – such visions as Virginia Woolf's (in *Three Guineas*, chapter 3, note 42) in which

LOVE & DEATH

The old conception that one sex must 'dominate' another would ... become not only obsolete, but so odious that if it were necessary for practical purposes that a dominant power should decide certain matters, the repulsive task of coercion and dominion would be relegated to an inferior and secret society, much as the flogging and execution of criminals is now carried out by masked beings in profound obscurity. But this is to anticipate.

OPEN SEASON ON WOMEN

OPEN SEASON ON WOMEN

THAT MEN are afraid of women is not – despite the headlines – news. Men will always be afraid of women, so long as patriarchy lasts, for the same reason that millionaires will always tremble at the thought of revolution. The master fears the slave. The slave might revolt. There does not seem to be any reason why women should not enslave men. Men have enslaved women for ten thousand years. If it is woman's turn now, who can have the gall to object? For that matter, woman still has a biological function to perform. Man is extinct. Insemination will require tomorrow only common salt and cheap electricity. Meanwhile, the bitch-heroine unrolls the blueprint. And woman preens & queens it, dreaming of the majesty that will be hers. And why not? Fantasy or fact, the bitch will prove difficult to dislodge. She has been attacked ten thousand times before. Attacked, and perhaps created.

It is necessary to distinguish between fair and unfair attacks, grievance and conscience, cause & effect. Like the good, rich burghers of Back Bay in the Boston police strike, sitting at their darkened windows with loaded shotguns to protect themselves from the 'mob' – said 'mob' being downtown at the time, busy stealing shoes – guilty men have been fleeing for centuries when no woman pursued. Socrates' homosexual apothegms turn up in Plato under the guise of philosophy. St. Paul's gall-&-wormwood misogyny appears in the New Testament as religion. The distillation of medieval gallantry's seamier side is to be found in the vomit of Renaissance attacks upon women, incomprehensible in the pages of Chaucer and Guevara and all the rest without reference to the overloaded gutful of cicisbeism and knight-errantry that preceded.

When we read that Horace Walpole called Mary Wollstonecraft a 'hyaena in petticoats' (letter to Hannah More, January 24th, 1795) for pleading for woman's right to be treated as human, it is relevant to inquire whether the opinion of a notorious homosexual on the subject of women is not more apt to be propaganda than considered judgment. Oscar Wilde's witty animadversions on the dullness of women

LOVE & DEATH

and the depravity of merely normal love were read off the books as merely special pleading the day he went to gaol. His stature as artist – whatever it may be – is not diminished by his homosexuality; he is simply warranted unfit by it to sit in judgment upon woman and normal love. His perspective – on the outside looking in – may have been the best in the world, but his candor is suspect. Similarly, Schopenhauer's fulminations against 'that under-sized, narrow-shouldered, broad-hipped, short-legged race' of women are recognized (like Nietzsche's and Weininger's suicidal screams) as the angry vaporings of a syphilitic discussing the sex that poured poison into his veins – a poison, as Ibsen understood, that some other man had poured into theirs.

Living writers cannot be brought before the bar of psychiatry and medicine, and required to give an account of themselves before they deliver impassioned tirades or publish feline attacks against one sex or the other. The libel laws do not permit such inquiry into their possible motives until after they are dead. But any writer's work may be analyzed for its propaganda content. And any writer who continually sets off sex against sex, any writer who persistently declares – openly or from ambush – that all women or all men are jinxes, looters, and murderers of the opposite sex, may properly and legally be asked if he (or she) is not suffering from at least an *idée fixe*, has not been harping years on end on the same single plucked-out string.

What, for instance, has W. Somerset Maugham been selling for fifty years and more, but one and the same story under a dozen yearly titles: Girl meets boy – girl destroys boy – end of story. This was the message in *Of Human Bondage* (victim: the author); this was the message of *Rain*, Maugham's adaptation of the Thaïs legend (victim in both cases: a clergyman); this was the message of *The Painted Veil* (victim: a scientist), of *The Circle* (victim: 'a distinguished politician'), of *The Constant Wife* (victim: a philandering husband), of *The Letter* (victim: a nobody), of a whole library of short stories (victim: everybody); while the hero of *The Moon & Sixpence* (Gauguin) is heroic precisely because he deserts his wife, child, and mistress, and goes off to Goona Goona to beat the native girls and paint. Is this 'realism,' is this monomania, or is this propaganda?

What is the invariable theme of James Hilton's popular sentimental tawdry? An embarrassingly sloppy imitator of Maugham, his message is the same: Women are the ruination of men. In *Lost Horizon* two men are actually forced to leave heaven – Utopia –

Shangri-La — at the insistence of a woman who treacherously turns into an old hag the moment heaven is irrevocably left behind. Aesop never wrote a clearer fable than that. In the book the two men are merely acquaintances; in the movie they were made brothers to explain their otherwise inexplicable mutuality. As a further concession to normality, the book's Miss Brinklow, 'a small, rather leathery' female missionary, blossoms out in the movie as Gloria Stone, a tubercular prostitute.

In *Knight Without Armour* a British spy in Russia tangles successfully with sinister Bolsheviks — on the pattern of Maugham's autobiographical *Ashenden, or The British Agent* — but loses his life trying to keep up with an eighteen-year-old girl: dancing, hill-climbing, and all that strenuous sort of thing. Even the Chevalier d'Eon's transvestist spying never came to such a sad end. In *We Are Not Alone* a kindly doctor befriends a refugee female and ends up hanged for the murder of his wife. Two at a blow, and as simple as that.

Rage in Heaven is flatly a study of paranoid homosexuality, the story of a man who enters into competition with his own wife for the affections of his best friend — under the names of 'boyishness' and 'hero worship,' terms occurring frequently throughout Mr. Hilton's work — and who is finally driven to madness and suicide (which he craftily makes appear like murder, and Leave *Him* to Heaven too) when the best friend prefers the wife. The motion picture made from this in 1941 by Mr. Christopher Isherwood was a failure, the actors going through their parts with evident repugnance; but it has recently been re-exhibited in hopes of getting off the nut under cover of the 'psychological' movie trend.

The Reverend Freemantle of *And Now Good-bye* is Hilton's Paphnuce — at second remove from Anatole France. Tempted by a chance female to leave his wife, child, and chapel à la *Moon and Sixpence,* and rush off with her to Vienna to compose (not paint), he is saved just in the nick of time by her being mangled to death in a railway accident before he has gotten up enough steam to consummate his sin. This makes him a hero.

Whatever is missing here of Maugham's Gauguin is caught up in *Good-bye Mr. Chips*. Explicitly a 'woman-hater,' Chips meets the one woman in his life at the age of forty-eight when she wantonly risks his life and sprains his ankle while mountain climbing — low temperatures and high peaks are standard in Mr. Hilton's books — and he has the courage to kill her, in this case through childbirth.

LOVE & DEATH

She dies like clockwork within a year and a half of their marriage, and Mr. Chips (a schoolmaster) is left happily flagellating and serving tea to little boys. Flushed with success Mr. Hilton re-issued the background of kindly old Chips as a three-shilling murder-mystery ('the known fact that the body lay in the locked gymnasium awaiting the inquest on the morrow gave them a particular thrill' – chapter 4) under the title of *Was It Murder?*

It was. These things are not history: they are fiction. They did not really happen: Mr. Hilton made them up out of his own head, and Alexander 'Half Goddess' Woollcott plugged them to the hilt in America. If they are propaganda, what are they propaganda for? At the very least for hatred, animosity, and mistrust between women & men.

•

No MODERN writer has taken the hatred of women farther than has Ernest Hemingway. As becomes the virile chap he is, Hemingway goes out to meet the enemy, and kills off the women in all his books (when they do not kill the men) or reserves for them a fate apparently worse than death: sexual frustration. That – in a literary sense, of course – Mr. Hemingway loves death, and loves it in a sex-substituted way, no rational person will attempt to deny. He has left the record of his love for killing, with all its nervous overtones of sexual prestige, too clearly in *Death in the Afternoon* (bull-killing, and the necrophil-sadistic "Natural History of the Dead") and on the *Green Hills of Africa*, somewhat sicklied o'er with the blood of kudu-antelope, guinea-hen, hyena, lion, reedbuck, rhinoceros, water-buffalo, teal, duck, oryx, impalla, eland, bushbuck, leopard, kongoni, and sable killed, *pour le sport*, by Mr. Hemingway.

Mr. Hemingway began as an ambulance driver in World War I, and seems to feel he has a great deal of killing to catch up with before he can take his position as a man among men. This exclusive and unremitting concern with the infliction of death and not of life makes it possible for him blandly to expurgate his *Green Hills of Africa* ('If I ever hit you I'll break your mucking jaw' – page 277) some years before the craven, dollar-a-word 'I obscenity in the obscenity of your obscenity' – as S. J. Perelman typifies it – of *For Whom the Bell Tolls*. It also makes it possible for him to prefix a haughty invitation for 'Any one not finding sufficient love interest ... while reading ... to insert whatever love interest he or she may have at the time.'

OPEN SEASON

Perhaps this is just a joke. Or perhaps it means that the reader is to alternate – on the style of the Marquis de Sade – between Mr. Hemingway's animal-killings and the consolations of love, as does Mr. Hemingway himself on page 66 ('Poor Karl... Without his wife') and, exceptionally, in the autobiographical "Fathers and Sons" in *Winner Take Nothing*. Or perhaps it just means that the author absorbed in death has no strength left for love – and perhaps this is just as well. Hemingway playing at literary love is (to paraphrase Kipling) more deadly than the Gatling gun.

His method – and perhaps his motives – have developed in clear order since his very first book. He begins by showing the tyrannous mother and theoretically unvirile father; continues with the 'native-girl' sexual outlet who has no rights and no status, and who is to keep her trap shut and be used, abused, and discarded exactly as the white man sees fit. This effortless, impersonal, nocturnal pollution the only sexual situation with which Hemingway's young man feels strong enough to cope, he is incapable of undertaking any adult relationship with woman as a human equal. He sees her always as matriarch and tyrant destroying him, and he must destroy her first in 'self-defense.'

Finally, woman being too strong for him, the Hemingway hero has no other recourse but – like Goldsmith's lovely woman who stooped to folly and found, too late, that men betray – to castrate himself, or turn homosexual, or die and thus punish her. Suicide as revenge. In order to make his loss the more deeply felt, however, he must first have had his woman climbing the walls with pleasure in his sexual prowess. She is then sure to miss him. This is the one & only aperture through which sex ever wriggles into Hemingway's writing, and it is on the basis of this obviously hateful hocus-pocus that his absurd *sub rosa* reputation as a 'hot' writer is based.

Edmund Wilson has analyzed Hemingway's slaughter of his female characters in *The Wound and the Bow* (an expurgated version appearing in the *Atlantic Monthly*, July 1939, with 'virility' for '*cojones*,' 'dirty dogs' for 'dirty bastards,' &c.) Let us complete the record here. It is not pretty. Not even as pretty as the endless spectacle of disembowelled horses and hyenas, and bulls and antelopes done in and dragged out, in which Mr. Hemingway takes such proselytizing delight.

In his first book, *In Our Time*, the Michigan boy in "The Doctor and the Doctor's Wife" – Hemingway is the son of a Michigan doctor – shows his father where he can find black squirrels to kill to compensate for the tyranny of his mother and the superior virility of the

LOVE & DEATH

Indian men. In "Now I Lay Me" (in *Men Without Women*), the early high point of Hemingway's interest in animal-sadism — bait-torturing and fish-killing — this same boy's mother burns up his father's arrowhead collection while he is away, naturally, on a hunting trip. In "Indian Camp" a 'damn squaw bitch' forces her husband into suicide by screaming too loudly during a Caesarean without anesthetic.

By contrast, in "Mr. and Mrs. Elliot" (personally expurgated by the author for re-publication in America) sexual love is made into a joke — the verb for coitus becoming 'they tried to have a baby' — and the author-husband, a he-virgin, tortures his sexually incompatible wife by making her type out his long poems. 'He was very severe about mistakes and would make her re-do an entire page if there was one mistake. She cried a good deal . . .'

Brett, Lady Ashley, in *The Sun Also Rises* is a classic bitch, and calls herself by that name; the only man free of her domination being a castrato, the narrator. In *Men Without Women* — note the title — "An Alpine Idyll" concerns a peasant who stows his wife's dead body in the woodshed until he can bury her, come spring, meanwhile using her jaw as a hook to hang his lantern on. He cannot explain his action.

"Fifty Grand" opens with a drunken prostitute shaming a prize-fighter out of a saloon for an anti-Semitic remark! Similarly, in Hemingway's recrucifixion of Christ in modern slang, "To-day is Friday" ('You see me slip the old spear into him?') much is made of the fact that 'the women' are all there watching him die. Again, in *God Rest You Merry, Gentlemen,* a boy castrates himself on Christmas day because of 'that awful lust' — a revised version of Christ's expiation for man's original (sexual) sin. Considering our censorship, it is lucky for Christianity that the victim of the world's most famous literary lynch *was* crucified and not castrated.

By now the pattern is quite clear: Hemingway's women purposely destroy their men; but men destroy women only helplessly, in reprisal, and as a last resort. To make women's motive crystal-clear, the principal admission of sexual pleasure in watching the bulls' *Death in the Afternoon* is put into the mouth of an 'old lady' — apparently a caricature of Gertrude Stein.

In *Winner Take Nothing* — 14 stories, 4 of them concerned with homosexuality — a drowned woman so unnerves the poor diver in "After the Storm" that he loses a fortune in salvage. No sympathy is requested for the dead woman. In "The Light of the World" a prostitute, under the influence of narcotics, fantasies that she has gotten a prize-fighter knocked out as he turns to smile at her. In "The Sea Change" a woman deserts her lover for a Lesbian vacation, promising to come back and rub his nose in all the details. This changes him into 'quite a different man.' What was unsatisfactory about him the way he was is not stated.

In "The Mother of a Queen" a homosexual bullfighter – the 'queen' – allows his mother's grave to be dug up and her bones dumped on the public boneheap. Why he is so lacking in love for his mother is also not stated. Perhaps she burned up his father's arrowhead collection. It has been known to happen. In "Homage to Switzerland" another homosexual tortures a waitress by offering her enormous sums of money to 'go upstairs' with him, though 'he knew there was no upstairs to go to.' Here, perhaps, hatred shades off into insanity.

In *The Fifth Column* the hero uses up all his dynamism killing human beings (Fascists: non-human), and has nothing left but contempt to offer the girl who wants to get in bed with him. She is too rich – i.e. too strong – too educated. Yet in *A Farewell to Arms* even abject docility cannot save the woman. Though only a hospital slavey, she is white, therefore a social equal and a probable danger. The hero kills her through childbirth (Mr. Chips' method), later finding sexual intercourse with her corpse unsatisfactory. In *To Have and Have Not* the hero-slaughterer (of non-human Cubans and Chinese) does it the other way, getting even with his woman – who is wildly pleased with his supersexuality – by dying and leaving her unsatisfied and presumably unsatisfiable, nature having broken the mould when he was made.

The early Hemingway stories leaned principally toward castration or the flight into homosexuality. The later revenge-technique of suicide is prefigured in "One Reader Writes" in *Winner Take Nothing* where a man gets 'sifilus' in China, leaving his faithful wife racked with sexual hunger. It is now repeated with fur-lined frills & trills in *For Whom the Bell Tolls,* the dynamitard-hero dying and leaving the previously raped, vegetable heroine – he calls her 'Rabbit' – vainly looking for someone else who can make 'the earth move' for her. There is even a *dybbuk* motif here, in that with his death this native-girl in her boyish haircut is no longer herself but the mere receptacle of the man's dead soul. The opposite female character, Pilar, is a horrendous mixture of shrew, cobra (page 173), and Xanthippe, nagging her man to actual death.

Yet all this murdering of & by women is not realism. It is not required by any inner structural necessity of Hemingway's stories. It is patently the fear & hate of women speaking more clearly than all his art. Edmund Wilson has seen the epitome and final convolution of Hemingway's agony in the short stories "The Snows of Kilimanjaro" and "The Short Happy Life of Francis Macomber":

> And now this instinct to get the women down presents itself frankly as a fear that the women will get the men down. The men in both these African stories are married to American bitches [*Atlantic Monthly*: harpies] of the most soul-destroying sort . . . 'Francis Macomber' perfectly realizes its purpose. Here the male saves his soul at the last minute, and then is actually shot down by his woman, who does not want him to have a soul. Here Hemingway has at last got what Thurber calls the war between the sexes right out into the open and has written a terrific fable of the impossible civilized woman who despises the civilized man for his failure in initiative and nerve, and then jealously tries to break him down as soon as he begins to exhibit any.

. . . Re-enter, the bitch.

●

OPENLY transvalued from sex, the death that Hemingway sells is frank and bold. He makes no pretense of 'mystery' behind his murders, no genuflection to law and justice, not even to lynch-law. He is out to kill because he is a *man*, and castrated death and frightened killing — he says — are man's work. Sex is presumably for homosexuals. Sex, when he writes of it, is dismal, unproductive; invariably the provocation for more death. He is out to kill, and he is out to kill women. Other animals will do as substitutes (even ants, as in *A Farewell to Arms*), but women are the chosen prey. In the face of a literary message like this, mystery-murders are nothing.

These men who propagandize for sex-hate are selling a more dangerous kind of violence than the murder-mystery can ever achieve. Their audience is the world, their victims half the human race. Three hundred straw-stuffed outlaws are done to death yearly in American murder-mysteries, perhaps twice as many more in Great Britain and Europe combined — a scant thousand in all, and all strictly as fantasy. But Maugham, Hilton, Hemingway, and their like are outlawing an entire, living sex — one billion human beings. Yearly they declare open season on women.

OPEN SEASON

And suddenly the virus takes. Suddenly the air is filled with shouting, with hoarse cries all around us: 'Women! The women did it! Women are barracudas! Kill all the women!' No longer do we hear that women are inferior, that women have no souls, no brains (only 'intuition'), no genius – have produced no great music, no art, no poetry. These are the sticks of yesteryear with which to beat the dog. The new anti-womanism abdicates everything, admits everything, throws itself on the mercy of the world. 'The women are coming! Save us, save us!'

But even in adapting this – Hitler's scapegoat technique – to the war between the sexes, the endless war to *keep women down*, men still have some shame. They hesitate to admit that they have played Frankenstein to their own monster – priding themselves on the possession of the best-decorated rag and bone and hank of hair in town, manufacturing the merest wallpaper of male ostentation out of what might have been women. They are ashamed to confess that they have grovelled and abased themselves before idols of their own creating: the frizzled wig, the painted face, the rubber teat, the girdled buttock, the silk-clad leg, the high-heeled foot. They are outraged that this same foot has felt its power, has turned and kicked them in the collective rump. They are afraid to acknowledge that even after ten thousand years of enslavement, woman – through the naked physical fact of man's need of her – is still strong enough to get her master down.

And so we are given to understand that this reversal of rôles is to be effected by stealth – by a sort of *Protocols of the Amazon Elders* – by perverted mothers, sapping the virility of their boy-babies in the cradle like so many French governesses. Forgetting Hemingway and the bitch-matriarch he has been beating up for twenty years, forgetting Swift, St. Paul, Strindberg, Santayana, and all the sonorous roll-call of anti-feminists of the past, the woman-murderers have a new prophet – a pulpitless pigmy-Jeremiah – a Mr. Philip Wylie.

Who is this Philip Wylie, to whose Damn-My-Mother banner (a word is expurgated here) our cheapjack editorialists are flocking, our publicity-needful psychologists are gathering the clan? In 1928, on page 143 of his first serious book, *Heavy Laden* (published by Knopf), Mr. Wylie had the guts to break off his love-scene with the cry: 'Now, damn you, take your row of dots.' There has not been an uncensored peep out of him since. He has found outlet elsewhere for his asterisked, unsaleable sex. He has written it blissfully into fish-killing, pyromania, prize-fighting, murder. And now, like a

LOVE & DEATH

frenzied ascetic, he throws himself upon women, in a verbigerous picture-gallery of bitches, epileptics, Jungians – sounding off in the souped-up journalese of a mezzobrow Westbrook Pegler on subjects the very nature of which is clearly beyond his panic-stricken mind. God's angry mite, he stands on literary street-corners shouting 'Doom! Doom! Doom!'

All but one of his lamentations fall upon deaf ears, but for this *one* a sudden, briskly nodding audience springs up. Women, educated women, and especially mothers, he lets us know – first in *Finnley Wren* and *The Bedroom Companion,* now in *Generation of Vipers* – women are the cause of the woeful gutlessness of modern men. Step right up, ladies & gentlemen, here she is: the most awful, the most dangerous, the most rootin'-tootin'est pistol-packin' mama in captivity – The Bitch-Mom! – Hemingway, Wylie & Co., purveyors.

In Europe the cry has been: When in doubt, kill the Jews! (Also in sex-pure Boston.) We are now learning to make woman the scapegoat. Rights? – Damn her. Equality? – Blast her! she's got too much already. Power, like the power men have got? – Kill her! Thus Mr. Hemingway, thus Mr. Wylie, thus all their weeping cohorts.

Women have their murder-fantasies too. They do not sprint down the street shouting 'Run for your lives, the dam is busted!' They sit home and read. Men have been attacking them since Eden – 'The woman ... she gave me of the tree, and I did eat.' Woman is now tired of taking the blame. She is tired of being murdered. She has had a bellyful of being the everlasting victim. Today she writes her own books (or Ben Ames Williams writes them for her) and these books say on every page and in every line, 'Kill all the men!' There is no time to squabble over who struck the first blow – who fed the apple to whom. It does not matter now whether Hemingway gave birth to Scarlett O'Hara, or Mary Wollstonecraft to Hemingway. The paper bitch is here, and she is reproducing herself in life in accordance with Oscar Wilde's staggering axiom – the gospel of all advertising – 'Life imitates Art.' And what is she selling under her 'historical' mask? Death? More than death: cannibalism. 'Kill them,' she whispers. 'Murder the murderers – fathers, husbands, sons. Gobble them up alive.'

•

DO NOT BE alarmed. It is not so easy to kill off half the human race. We must either kill *every*body, and arrange for there to be no more, or both sexes must go back to their murder-pap fantasies. (Doubling in brass, Messrs. Hemingway & Wylie are selling these too.) Or perhaps we can combine both alternatives in one great sexless paean to death. For this we must train up every generation afresh to murder and to hate – to death but never to love. A toy gun at three. Bang, bang. A soldier-suit at four. Bang, bang, bang. Boxing gloves at five. Too cute for words! But for 'self-abuse,' loud lectures, whippings, and supperless sendings to bed, the guilty arms immobilized in cardboard tubes.

Then books and movies and radio, razzle-dazzling the eyes & ears with blood and violence – with cowboy killers, pirates, train-wrecks – at every critical moment when, without these innocent diversions ('divert: to change the aim or purpose of . . . as children are diverted with sports'), sex might be experimented with. We need 'comic'-books in three colors and black, selling death and torture – five hundred million yearly. Superprig in the 60th century, a ray-gat blazing in each mitt, doing in his country's enemies a thousand at a clip, knocking out a tooth with every patriotic knuckle. Noble tales of death and derring-do are needed. The pavements are gray. Our days are drab. We must fill them with dreams of murder flying through the air. The monster, sex, is waiting for our children if we falter.

Repeat the glorious saga: how we killed the dastardly redskins for living in the homes we wanted, how cleverly we gypped them out of Manhattan with twenty-three dollars' worth of glass beads. There! there! there! – and another non-human bites the dust. My dear fellow, it is not easy to take the adolescent's mind off sex. It takes death, death, death, and more death. For adults, more still.

It takes twelve-part serials at the movies every Saturday – special for the kiddies – radio blather screaming before supper every day, with one or another grisly, flaming horror left impending at the end of every chapter. It takes religious organizations publishing murder-mysteries for the 'juvenile' trade, perhaps even Chesterton's reverend lyncher, Father Brown. It takes twenty-five million murder-magazines a year. It takes pictures of Mussolini hanging by his ankle like a slaughtered pig, photographs of Goering in the morgue so we can gloat over the death he cheated us out of. It takes headline after daily headline of death, but never a headline of love unless purified by murder, or by the touch of some actress, some millionaire, some demi-god.

Four million acts of intercourse are achieved in America daily. (Dr. Robert L. Dickinson: *Control of Conception*, 1938, page 1.)

OPEN SEASON

Figure it out for yourself. Is it news? Not news that's fit to print. But if two rachitic orphans should be killed by a falling wall in a jerry-built tenement, the pictures of their mangled corpses – of no interest whatever in sickly life – are spread over every news-sheet in the country in the name of 'human interest.' It takes this. It takes this and more. It takes – and here the camera stops – it takes a yearly, well-advertised fraud (this year the Shmook, last year Kilroy; always the same prick & balls) to figleaf the pinnacle of our success: a small boy chalking bawdy words and ugly invitations on a wall, spewing out the hatred we have taught him. *Es ist vollbracht.* It is consummated. Transvalued. Violence and death have saved us from sex.

Editors, publishers, policemen, lawyers, judges, and jailers – even a few writers – have become accustomed to the legal absurdity that, in writing of sex, the theoretical incitement to commit a misdemeanor – masturbation or coitus – is punished as a felony. Nowhere else at law does even the provable incitement to any offense carry with it a graver penalty than the offense itself.

But we have become accustomed to an even more significant absurdity, nailed four centuries ago in Montaigne's essay "On Some Verses of Virgil" (1588) book 3, chapter 5:

> We bravely say (Montaigne reminds us) kill, rob, betray; but that other we dare pronounce only between clenched teeth?

Murder is a crime. Describing murder is not. Sex is not a crime. Describing sex *is*. Why? The penalty for murder is death, or lifelong imprisonment – the penalty for writing about it: fortune and lifelong fame. The penalty for fornication is... there is no actual penalty – the penalty for describing it in print: jail and lifelong disgrace. Why this absurd contradiction? Is the creation of life really more reprehensible than its destruction?

Explanations are offered. The murder-mystery, the comic-book, the tabloid, picture-mag, prize-fight, horror-show – we are told – are the policeman's little helpers: cyanide lollypops to pacify the killer in us all. Then why is not pornography the clergyman's little friend? If reading about death will siphon off all our murderousness into nowhere, and cure us of killing, why would not reading about fornication cure us of sex? In books the murderer is always caught – the fornicators all could die of syphilis. Open the gates!

LOVE & DEATH

Or, contrariwise, if reading *is* ideomotor, if he & she who read of sex will try it out when no one is watching, why will not they who read of murder try that too when they have the chance? Why is the description of an act of love sure to excite its readers to rape, when the grisliest possible descriptions of death, in print and word and picture, cannot possibly excite anyone to murder? We protect ourselves so well from sex; why this flirtation with exciting us to cruelty and killing? Is our future to be more and more policemen restraining the incubated murderers of more and more tabloids, of more and more murder-mysteries, comic-books, picture-mags, movies, radio & television horror; protecting us from the breast-fed whelps of more and more bitch-heroines?

No, say calmer minds, crime & punishment are balanced against the *price* of fantasy & fact. The penalty for murder is so grave – except in war – that even the most avid reader of its lynch and bitch details will shrink from emulation. But the penalty for fornication is so minor that reading of it might tempt untold innocents to its performance. Here, then, we have the final absurdity. We are renting out murder, selling in fantasy our most forbidden crime to five, ten, fifty million customers a year; while prohibiting the appearance – even in fantasy – of our least forbidden misdemeanor.

But let us not make Milton's mistake – pleading for free speech with one hand, and writing the censor's *damnatur* with the other. No one suggests that the sale of blood and murder should be stopped. No one, that is, except Dr. Wilhelm Reich (*The Sexual Revolution*, 1945, page 262) and one defunct law; and they want 'pornography' prohibited too. No one suggests that sex should replace death, instead of the traditional reverse. But perhaps we could have them both together. Perhaps one would work its leaven upon the other. Let us have our death. For God's sake, let us have our death! Deforest Canada for paper-pulp if you must, but give us this day our daily death.

Brandes, writing his *Hovedstrømninger* today, would find only one main current in our literature – deathward. On, to the pit! Well, we have been warned. Mené-mené-tekál-&-murder was never written larger on any wall. We are travelling toward death. We love it, we want it, and we are going to get it. Sex – the opposite of death – may or may not save us. But we cannot hold back the flood with institutionalized amok.